General editor: Graham Handley

Brodie's Notes on Shelagh Delaney's

A Taste of Honey

John Jenkins
Lecturer in English, East Devon College

Pan Books London, Sydney and Auckland

Extracts from *A Taste of Honey*
© Shelagh Delaney 1958
Published by Methuen Inc and reproduced by
permission of Tessa Sayle Agency
First published 1988 by Pan Books Ltd,
Cavaye Place, London SW10 9PG
9 8 7 6 5 4 3 2 1
© Pan Books Ltd 1988
ISBN 0 330 50272 7
Photoset by Parker Typesetting Service, Leicester
Printed and bound in Great Britain by
Richard Clay Ltd, Bungay, Suffolk

Contents

References in these notes are to
the Methuen Student edition of
A Taste of Honey but as each
scene is analysed separately, the Notes
may be used with any edition of the book.

Preface

The intention throughout this study aid is to stimulate and guide, to encourage the reader's *involvement* in the text, to develop disciplined critical responses and a sure understanding of the main details.

Brodie's Notes provide a summary of the plot of the play or novel followed by act, scene or chapter summaries, each of which will have an accompanying critical commentary designed to emphasize the most important literary and factual details. Poems, stories or non-fiction texts will combine brief summary with critical commentary on either individual aspects or sequences of the genre being considered. Textual notes will be explanatory or critical (sometimes both), defining what is difficult or obscure on the one hand, or stressing points of character, style, plot or the technical aspects of poetry on the other. Revision questions will be set at appropriate points to test the student's careful application to the text of the prescribed book.

The second section of each of these study aids will consist of a critical examination of the author's art. This will cover such major elements as characterization, style, structure, setting, theme(s) for example in novels, plays or stories; in poetry it will deal with the types of poem, rhyme, rhythm, free verse for example, or in non-fiction with the main literary concerns of the work. The editor may choose to examine any aspect of the book being studied which he or she considers to be important. The paramount aim is to send the student back to the text. Each study aid will include a series of general questions which require detailed knowledge of the set book: the first of these questions will have notes by the editor of what *might* be included in a written answer. A short list of books considered useful as background reading for the student will be provided at the end.

The author and her work

Shelagh Delaney was born in 1939 in Salford, Manchester, where *A Taste of Honey* is set. She failed the 11+ examination which would have enabled her to get into the grammar school, and attended Broughton Secondary School instead. It was at Broughton School that she saw her first play – an amateur performance of Shakespeare's *Othello*. She was twelve at the time, and the play made a great impression on her, so great in fact that she has Jimmie quote some lines from it to Jo in *A Taste of Honey*. At fifteen, she was transferred to the grammar school where she passed five O levels. After leaving school, she held a variety of jobs in Salford – shop assistant, clerk in a milk depot, usherette – but it was always her ambition to write.

When she was seventeen, she began *A Taste of Honey* as a novel but realized that it would be better as a play. The reason she gives for changing from the novel to drama is interesting; she objected to the way 'North Country people are shown as gormless, whereas in actual fact they are very alive and cynical' (quoted from an interview with Laurence Kitchen, 1959). She saw a production of a play entitled *Variations on a Theme* by Terence Rattigan which she considered bland and trivial, and was convinced that she could do better. So she took a fortnight off work to adapt her novel into a play.

In 1958, *A Taste of Honey* was accepted by Joan Littlewood, a famous director, who strongly believed that plays should be about ordinary people, not the genteel middle-classes portrayed by writers like Rattigan. It opened in the East End of London in May 1958, transferring to the West end early the following year, where it enjoyed a long run and won several awards. The critic and film director Lindsay Anderson called it 'A work of complete, exhilarating originality.' In 1960 *A Taste of Honey* was staged in New York and won a drama prize. Two years later Shelagh Delaney wrote the screenplay for the film version which won an Academy Award. At the age of 23, she had become one of the most famous writers of her time.

Since then her writing has shown remarkable versatility. In 1963, she produced a collection of short stories entitled *Sweetly*

Sings the Donkey, several television plays (among them *Did your Nanny Come from Bergen? (1970)*, and *St Martin's Summer* (1974)), award-winning filmscripts such as *Charley Bubbles* and *Dance with a Stranger* (1982), and radio plays such as *So Does the Nightingale* (1980).

However, it is still *A Taste of Honey* that is Shelagh Delaney's best-known work. As you study the play, remember that at the time she wrote it she was not much older than Jo. It was therefore that much easier for her to identify with and understand the problems of an unhappy teenager. This is not to say that she was unhappy herself – in fact, Shelagh Delaney has said that when she started *A Taste of Honey* as a novel she was too busy enjoying herself going dancing to work systematically at it. But if it was easy to identify with Jo, it would also have been easy to sentimentalize her, and Shelagh Delaney does not do this. Jo exists as a fully-rounded, complex person, not as a projection of the writer's teenage fantasies. You might find that you know someone very like Jo. Even if you do not, Shelagh Delaney's presentation of her makes it easy for us to understand her anxieties and confusion as well as her strength of character.

In your reading of the play, you should also be constantly aware of the humour. Sometimes it is difficult when reading a play on your own or in class to appreciate the comedy which a performance of the play makes immediately clear. Remember that although *A Taste of Honey* is serious and even sombre on occasions, it is also very funny. Look for examples of humour, and even broad slapstick comedy, not only in the dialogue, but in the stage directions which give an idea of what the characters are doing rather than what they are saying.

You will find yourself responding more fully to the play if you never forget that it is a play; a dramatic experience which is not to be confused with real life. Your attention will be drawn to this in the scene-by-scene Commentaries and the section entitled Location. However, as you read through the play you might find it useful to note those occasions when attention is drawn to its artificiality. This artificiality – in such things as dancing and singing – is all the more important because the dialogue is so authentic that it would be easy to view the play as a 'slice of life'.

Try to remember these points – the humour, the emphasis upon its being a play, and the authenticity of its dialogue – and you will find that you enjoy the play more as well as understanding it better.

Scene commentaries, textual notes, revision questions and assignments

Act 1 Scene 1

Pages 7–16

This section covers the opening of the play up to the time that Peter enters.

From the start we are made aware of the kind of relationship that exists between Jo and Helen. These first moments, too, provide us with important clues about the kind of play that Shelagh Delaney has written. We notice almost immediately that Jo feels let down by her mother, and has a strained relationship with her. She is disappointed that the flat her mother has found is so shabby and comfortless; she is determined to find somewhere of her own as soon as she can, and is disgusted by her mother's heavy drinking. Her remark about her mother being a prostitute of sorts shows a blatant lack of respect, and, at the same time gives us a valuable insight into Helen's nature and background. Like many young people of her age, Jo finds herself at odds with her mother and makes no attempt to moderate her criticism of her.

Helen, for her part, shows a willingness to accept the squalor of the flat, which Jo finds intensely annoying. Whereas Helen can joke about it, Jo is offended by the ugliness of the flat and wraps her scarf around the unshaded light bulb in an attempt to make the place more homelike. In other words, Helen, unlike her daughter, has become accustomed to living in cheap, poorly furnished accommodation and sharing a bed with her. Although she tells Jo that she is careful, we feel from the outset that she is not, and Jo herself confirms this a little later when she accuses Helen of acting without thinking. She accepts whatever life offers, unable or unwilling to make plans of any kind. This flat is merely one like many others she has lived in; she has no expectation of anything better.

As we read the first few pages, we feel, too, that their undisguised hostility to each other is the normal register of their relationship. This is confirmed by the insults and accusations which ebb and flow between the two of them, neither really seeming to be hurt by what the other says. They are hurt, of course, but feel it would indicate weakness to show it. Their relationship seems to be unpunctuated by any show of the affection usual between a mother and daughter.

Two of Jo's early speeches give us a possible clue to what kind of play this is. Its dialogue is obviously realistic, and captures very convincingly the way people's conversation wanders from one point to the next. But both of the main characters talk, at various times, *about* the other rather than *to* her (using 'she' rather than 'you'). Of course, people sometimes talk in this way to show their exasperation, although they are not actually speaking to anyone. But since this is a play, it is possible that such comments are directed at the audience. If we think about this for a moment, we will see that by doing so, Shelagh Delaney is drawing our attention to the artificiality of the play. Actors do not usually address remarks to the audience because it would spoil the illusion of reality which the play tries to create, but maybe this is exactly what Shelagh Delaney wants to do; that is, make us aware that this is a piece of theatre not a piece of real life. You might find it helpful as you read through the play to mark the occasions when a character seems to speak to the audience.

As we begin to settle into the play, and become aware of the characters of the two people introduced so far, Shelagh Delaney adds to the details of their personalities. We notice, for example, Helen's preoccupation with her cold, and her impatience with Jo (although she is clearly looking for some sympathy from her daughter). This gives us a glimpse of the kind of mother Helen is. She is rarely deliberately nasty or cruel, merely careless and self-absorbed, and perhaps needs her daughter more than she cares to admit. We notice, too, Jo's total lack of interest in Helen's cold; she never once responds to Helen's complaints. But the self-absorption of Helen and the deliberate callousness of Jo are relieved for a moment by a comic incident, when Jo lights the stove, which is a moment of pure slapstick.

If you look carefully at the conversation which follows – about the man Jo liked – you will see that Jo and Helen have now exchanged roles for a while. Helen becomes deliberately callous and Jo self-absorbed. It is a good example of the fluid nature of their relationship. Jo reminisces about one of Helen's boyfriends whom she liked. She does not respond directly to any of her mother's questions, and voices her thoughts almost as if Helen is not there. Helen, however, soon identifies the man, and then makes some seemingly cruel comments to the audience about how upset Jo was when he ran off with a landlady's daughter. This episode reveals a longing in Jo for romantic love which is an important development in her character and increases our sympathy for her. So far, she has appeared independent and even callous. In this incident, her guard drops for a moment, and we see her as vulnerable and wishing for love.

We are then given a further reminder of the sordid surroundings in which they live. Yet although Helen complains about the ugliness around her she does nothing to improve it. Shelagh Delaney uses this to develop a contrast between mother and daughter which she has already suggested. Jo wishes to make the flat a little more colourful and homely, and has stolen some bulbs from the park. This is an important episode because while it shows Helen's careless attitude as a mother, it also suggests certain basic differences between mother and daughter. Helen seems not to care particularly whether Jo steals or not. Nor does she show any interest in the bulbs although they are clearly quite important to Jo. We learn, too, that Jo has tried to grow bulbs in other flats they have rented. It seems from this that Jo needs beauty more than her mother does. Perhaps what we are witnessing here is a conscious attempt on Jo's part to develop a personality and tastes of her own, distinct and different from Helen's.

The conversation continues in what we now recognize as a typically insulting tone which leads to Helen recalling her first job in a pub and singing a snatch of a song. For a moment or two the abrasive tone softens, for her memory is a happy one, a pleasant memory which frees her from the ugliness and the anxieties of the present. We notice, too, that she addresses the orchestra in the theatre, asking them to play along with her. By doing so, she once again breaks the illusion of realism in the play, just as she and Jo have already done by speaking to the audience.

The moment of sweet remembrance soon passes, however, and the sharper tone of mutual insult between mother and daughter is re-established. They seem to take pleasure in belittling and hurting each other.

Helen's discovery of Jo's drawings and her surprise at the

talent they show reveals her previous lack of interest in her daughter's education and abilities. Jo's reluctance to let her mother see the drawings is further evidence of her fierce wish for independence from Helen. She cannot resist the opportunity to blame her mother for her poor, unsettled education, and abruptly dismisses Helen's suggestion that she should go to art school.

Helen's offer to pay for Jo's training reveals another side to her character. Behind the insults and apparent lack of interest there lies a concern for her daughter. We do not question the sincerity of her offer to pay. What we do question are her ability to pay, and, assuming her ability, her consistent determination to do so. Fixity of purpose does not seem to be one of her most prominent characteristics, as we see both from Jo's complaints and Helen's own admissions about herself. We can understand why Jo is anxious to leave her mother, and live a more settled life of her own.

Pages 16–22

This section covers the scene from the entry of Peter until the close. Shelagh Delaney delays the entry of her third character, Peter, until she has firmly established her two principal characters and presented us with a clear idea of the kind of people they are and how they get on with each other. The music which plays as Peter enters is yet another reminder of the theatrical nature of the play. It is rather like a variety show where each celebrity comes onto the stage to a signature tune. The stage-direction describing Peter is brief, but gives us an immediate idea of what he is like. He seems to be something of a stereotype salesman – showy, confident, swaggering.

His entrance certainly has an effect on both Helen and Jo. Jo immediately suspects that Helen's reason for moving to the flat was to escape from Peter, but we never discover if this is true. She takes an instant dislike to him, and is reluctant to leave her mother alone with him, even though Peter makes it brutally clear that he wants Jo out of the way. There are two possible reasons why Jo does not want to do as Helen asks and leave her alone with Peter. The obvious one is that by staying, Jo can spite her mother. A less obvious, but very powerful motive is that she sees in Peter a rival for her mother's affection. Up to the entrance of Peter, Jo has been hostile to her mother. Now she competes with Peter for her attention, and so another aspect of Jo's character emerges here. Although she is highly critical of her mother, she is nevertheless bound to her by strong ties of custom, and having no father perhaps needs Helen rather more than she would like to admit. Part of Peter's function as a character here, then, is to allow Shelagh Delaney to show us Jo's emotionally confused attitude towards Helen.

Peter's entrance brings about a change in Helen too. Shortly before he came in, she had shown some interest in Jo's drawings. Earlier still, we had seen her looking to Jo for sympathy because she is suffering from a cold. Now her attention focuses exclusively on Peter. Jo has become an unwanted presence. This kind of fickleness obviously hurts Jo and shows how selfish Helen can be.

For his part, Peter displays a remarkable degree of insensitivity when he begins to fondle Helen actually in the presence of her daughter. When Jo eventually leaves to make some coffee, we are given a little scene which shows us how weak and suggestible Helen is with brash, confident men. At first, we notice that she is anything but warm and welcoming to Peter. But gradually she begins to yield to his charm as he mixes comically suggestive comments with a joking offer of marriage. Despite herself, Helen finds that she responds to him, not so much to his proposal, which she does not seem to take too seriously, as to his sexual attractiveness and his obvious desire for her. It is worth reading the section carefully because it shows how Helen's physical impulses are stronger than her mental will.

Although Peter twice mentions marriage to Helen, he never says that he loves her. He does, however, find her sexually attractive, and it is upon sexual attraction and having a good time that their relationship is based. They certainly share several interests: drink, dirty jokes and sex among them.

When Jo re-enters with the coffee, the mood of the scene hardens once more. Helen actually attributes Jo's moodiness to jealousy at seeing her mother showing affection to someone else. Jo's barbed response helps confirm our impression that although she professes to be immune to her mother's behaviour, she in fact feels hurt, betrayed and angry at the attention Helen has shown to her boyfriends but has denied her own daughter. This is well captured in the incident when Peter pulls Helen to him, embraces her, and then tells her a dirty story. It is all done in front of Jo, who constantly interrupts them by asking questions and making provocative comments. She feels rejected and so seeks attention. If you picture the scene in your mind, you will see how the grouping of the characters helps to emphasize this rejection. Helen is enfolded in Peter's embrace at the door to the flat. Jo is physically separate from them, sitting on her own and observing.

After Peter leaves, the scene draws to a close with the usual acrimonious exchanges between mother and daughter, although these are leavened by a little tenderness which Helen shows toward Jo at the end. A likely reason for this gentleness is that Helen is about to introduce a sensitive topic – marriage. The way she does so suggests that she is rather hesitant and perhaps even looking for Jo's approval. We note, too, that although Helen did not seem to take Peter's proposal seriously earlier in the scene, she has evidently been thinking about it since then.

By the time Scene 1 ends we have come to realize that the relationship between Helen and Jo is not as straightforward as it seemed at first. There is negligence on Helen's part, and genuine youthful rebellion on Jo's. Yet for all the hostility they display there is, almost despite themselves, a link between them which is stronger than either of them seem to realize.

Jazz music The jazz music might be coming from the street outside. However as we become more familiar with the play we see that music often accompanies the entrance of characters onto the stage, in rather the same way that it does entertainers in cabaret or on the television.

When I find somewhere . . . the rent Several of Helen's comments to Jo reveal her sarcastic wit.

When you start earning you can start moaning One of several of Helen's comments which have a proverbial flavour, and draw our attention to the realism of the dialogue.

contemporary A term applied in the 1950s to clothes as well as furnishings. Contemporary design at that time used bold, sharply contrasting colours and angular shapes.

She'd lose her head if it was loose A slang expression meaning that someone is careless or forgetful.

Then get it down you! Drink it!

shilling in the slot affairs A shilling (5 pence) placed in the slot of a gas meter bought a certain number of units of gas for a cooker or a heater.

part of the furniture and fittings Items of furniture and utilities supplied by the landlord. Notice that Helen moves into a furnished flat because she owns no furniture of her own.

I don't know. Oh! It'll turn up Helen's failure here to complete the task she undertakes and actually find the heater is typical of her approach to life generally.

knocking it back Drinking.

Why can't you leave things alone? . . . third hanky today Notice how closely this echoes the way people actually talk. Helen shifts abruptly from one topic to another.

It's the only redeeming feature in this entire lodging house Helen's vocabulary here, and elsewhere as we shall see, that although she is careless and wayward, she is not stupid.

Perhaps he's one of the fixtures Perhaps he's supplied by the landlord as part of the flat. An example of Helen's rather bawdy humour.

fancy men Lovers.

a sight for sore eyes A colloquial term which usually means a pleasant, happy sight. Helen is being sarcastic here.

without giving shelter to the four winds Much of the language of the play is in the form of vigorous, colourful colloquialism of which this is a good example.

knocked me into the middle of next week Hit me very hard.

set on Determined to.

vamp it Play an improvised musical accompaniment.

It takes me all my time to look after myself Yet two pages earlier, Helen reprimanded Jo for being inconsiderate and putting herself first. A contradiction like this one adds greatly to the realism of Helen's character. She speaks as she feels at the moment, without any regard for consistency.

Go and see to that coffee When Jo said earlier that she intended making coffee, Helen was not interested whether she made it or not. Now she demands some. It's the kind of thing we all do, but it helps us to understand why Helen irritates Jo.

He would show up just when I've got her hanging round my neck A notable instance of the way Helen regards Jo as an obstacle to her full enjoyment of life.

Turn yourself into a bloody termite . . . make yourself scarce Although she regularly insults her daughter, the brutality of this remark is not typical of Helen. She speaks this way because she has been caught unawares by Peter, is embarrassed by Jo's presence (because it gives Peter a good idea of her real age) and so turns on her daughter.

classy Choosy.

kid A term of affection. It was popular in 'tough-guy' films of the time.

The only consolation I can find . . . your ultimate absence The sharp wit of Helen's comment contrasts with the harsh insult she hurled at Jo a moment or two earlier.

I told you I was throwing my hand in I told you I had finished with you.

the old firm A long-standing, well-established partnership.

Well, put your hat on . . . make an honest woman of you Peter's
proposal of marriage seems to be quite spontaneous. Like Helen, and
Jo too, he does not seem to consider the consequences of what he says
or does.

Now you know I like this mother and son relationship Peter is
jokingly referring to the difference in their ages, but this comment
draws our attention to the way in which Jo sees Peter as an opponent
for her mother's attention.

'Walter, Walter, lead me to the altar!' The title and first line of a
popular song.

The world is littered with women . . . less seemly virtues Peter is
obviously a boastful character, but notice, too, the polished way he
speaks here. Witty, elegant turns of phrase are part of his repertoire as
an experienced 'lady's man'.

'I see a quiet place, a fireplace, a cosy room' A line from a song
entitled *My Blue Heaven* which was popular at the time.

tap room The bar of a public house.

**I should have thought their courtship had passed the stage of
symbolism** The witty tone of this remark reminds us of Helen's to
Peter a little earlier – 'The only consolation . . . ultimate absence' – and
reminds us that for all her desire to be as different from her mother as
possible, Jo shares many of Helen's characteristics.

You want to be careful . . . coal black mammy's thigh's been Jo's witty
remark neatly punctures Peter's boastful claim.

the cat's been on the strawberries An obscure saying. Perhaps Peter
means that he won't be back because Jo (the cat) makes him feel
unwelcome.

It's dark out there now . . . you'll have to try a bit harder, won't you?
Notice how Helen manoeuvres Jo into a position where she can make
her callous remark 'Then you'll have to try . . .' Presumably Helen
wishes here to pay Jo back for her behaviour when Peter was there.

Everything is seen at its best in the dark In the dark, Helen finds
temporary escape from the sordidness of her surroundings and
reminders that she is growing older. It is a touching moment because
it shows that Helen is not as brash and uncaring as she sometimes
appears to be.

It's the darkness inside houses that I don't like Because houses are
associated with families. For Jo, such darkness magnifies her
uncertainty about her own present and future family life.

institution A mental home.

Questions and assignments on Act 1 Scene 1

1 Briefly, in a paragraph, write a factual account of what we are
told about the flat and its surroundings.

2 Write a brief account of what you have learned about Jo up to the time that Peter enters.

3 What have you discovered about Helen *and* Peter from the way in which they behave towards each other?

4 Make a list of those similarities and differences between Jo and Helen which you have noticed in the scene. Here are a couple to get you started:

Similarities	Differences
both women sharp-tongued	Helen careless about condition of flat.
	Jo strongly dislikes it.

5 Read through the scene again and write down those occasions when the characters might be speaking to the audience.

6 Do you find the relationship between Helen and Jo convincingly presented?

Assignments

1 Compare Jo's attitude towards her mother in this scene with that of any other character towards his or her mother or father in any book you have read.

2 Imagine that you are Jo. Write an account of Helen as you see her in this scene.

3 Jo feels jealous of the attention her mother pays to Peter. Describe an occasion when you felt jealous because you thought that someone was not paying you enough attention.

Act 1 Scene 2
Pages 22–26

This section deals with the scene between Jo and her boyfriend, Jimmie.

When we see Jo with Jimmie at the start of the scene, we remember that in Act 1 Scene 1 she told Helen she has never had a boyfriend. She might have been lying, of course, and keeping him secret from her mother in the same way that she kept her drawings secret. If this was so, we can quite understand that she feels the need for some kind of private life. After all, there is not much privacy in the flat she shares with her mother. On the other hand, it might be that enough time has passed since the end of the previous scene for her to meet her boyfriend.

We see another side to Jo in this section. So far she has been in almost perpetual conflict, mainly with her mother, but also with Peter. Now we see her in a more relaxed mood, snatching a moment or two of happiness with her boyfriend. From being someone who is unwanted in Scene 1, she is someone who is desired. Jimmie seems to be attracted to her partly because of her disregard for conventional social customs. She does not care what people think of her, and her rebelliousness seems to excite him. If we think carefully about this, we begin to wonder if she is attracted to Jimmie because of his colour. In the 1950s, when the play was written, mixed relationships were rare and less acceptable than they are now, so perhaps it is one way Jo feels she can show herself to be different from other people.

Jimmie's proposal of marriage is as much of a surprise to us as Peter's to Helen was, although the circumstances are entirely different. Whereas Helen at first brushed aside Peter's proposal, the joking style of Jo's acceptance shows her happiness at being asked. We notice, too that Jimmie asks her again, as if he cannot believe his good fortune. The freshness and joy they show contrast strongly with the soiled, sordid way in which Peter and Helen behave toward each other. We cannot, for instance, imagine Peter being so blissfully happy at Helen's acceptance that he would swing her through the air. It would be out of keeping with the debonair, suave image he tries to cultivate. What Shelagh Delaney shows with Jo and her boyfriend is the ecstatic happiness of which youth is capable.

We share in their happiness but if we give a moment's thought to what is happening, we might find that we also have doubts about the wisdom of the coming marriage. For one thing, we know little about her boyfriend. Although he says he adores her – and probably does when he says it – the other relationships we have seen so far in the play (Helen/Jo; Helen/Peter; Peter/Jo) do not make us optimistic about this one. We feel that perhaps Jo is snatching at happiness without fully understanding herself. For another thing, she is extremely young to become engaged. She tells her boyfriend that she is nearly eighteen, but the school-leaving age in the 1950s was fifteen, and so it is likely that Jo is not yet sixteen.

As if to emphasize Jo's youth and personal confusion, Shelagh Delaney introduces two incidents which show how unready Jo and Jimmie are for something as demanding as marriage. The first concerns the toy car Jimmie pulls from his pocket. Jo shows a child-like fascination with it and her behaviour here is a vivid reminder that in many important respects she is younger than her age. Having been denied a settled, loving upbringing, Jo has also been denied the chance of being a child, and here we see her seizing the opportunity when it presents itself. Naturally, we sympathize with her, but at the same time we see how unready she is, emotionally, for marriage.

The second example occurs almost immediately after, when Jimmie has tied the ring around her neck. She resolves to keep it tucked away because she thinks Helen will laugh at it. Yet a couple of pages earlier, Jo had given the impression that she did not care about what people thought of her, and Jimmie was convinced that she meant it. But clearly she does care what her mother would say about the engagement ring. What Shelagh Delaney is showing here is the contradictory nature of Jo's attitude towards her mother, and, more generally, how confused she is about her own personality. She likes to appear confident and unconventional, but we sense that on a deeper level she is very unsure of herself.

This leads us on to think about why Jo wishes to marry. Of course, one reason is that she believes she is in love with Jimmie. Her idea of love, however, is a very romantic one, as we can see from the large statements she makes about it. In fact, she has only the haziest notions of what love is. In her use of clichés lies her desperate yearning to be loved and wanted, and this is another reason why she wishes to marry. She not only wants to feel the joy of being in love, she craves to be loved herself, and Jimmie's affectionate behaviour satisfies this craving. Her attitude is a very understandable one when we consider how starved of care and attention she has been, but her need for romantic fulfilment does make her vulnerable.

Jo might have another reason – besides love – for wanting to marry: it will demonstrate her independence of Helen. Her engagement to Jimmie seems to be as much an act of self-assertion against her mother as a full-blooded commitment to her fiancé. Yet we note once more that even while she is expressing independence of her mother, Jo is quick to boast that Helen is not prejudiced against colour – wrongly as it happens. A little earlier, she had been anxious to assert her independence from her mother. Now she is eager to be fair to her.

As the scene between them continues, they talk about the time that Jimmie nearly seduced her. Although the tone of their conversation is happy, we begin to question Jimmie's motives for buying Jo a ring. Perhaps he really does adore her as he says. Perhaps he thinks she is more likely to let him seduce her if she thinks he intends to marry her. Perhaps he is not entirely sure of his own motives. This is something Shelagh Delaney leaves for us to decide. Certainly, he does not appear to be a womaniser like Peter. Even though both men wish to sleep with their partners, there is a tenderness in Jimmie's relationship with Jo which is lacking in Peter's with Helen.

Jo's need to romanticize her boyfriend reappears when she asks if his ancestors came from Africa. His reply – that they came from Cardiff – flatly demonstrates the gulf between the dreams she has of him and the ordinary person he actually is. Even then, she says she likes him because he has a wild, untamed streak in him. We wonder if this love of wildness is another characteristic she shares with her mother.

As their scene together draws to a close, we become aware that neither of them have seriously considered the practical problems of getting married. Jimmie jokingly warns Jo that she must make all kinds of sacrifices because they are saving up to get married. Then we learn that he is going drinking with his friends. Jo accepts this without question, not even suggesting lightheartedly that perhaps he should make sacrifices also.

Pages 26–29

This section deals with the departure of Jimmie and the scene between Jo and Helen.

The stage direction showing the departure of Jimmie, and the entrance of Helen and Jo is important because it emphasizes once more the music-hall nature of much of the play. Jimmie actually sings to the audience before leaving, and Jo and Helen dance on to music. It is another reminder of the artificiality of the characters and action.

While the conversation of Helen and Jo wanders realistically from topic to topic, it is given coherence by a common theme: men. Jo's dreamy entry immediately arouses Helen's suspicion. When she tells Helen a little about her boyfriend, both women think of their ideal male. We notice that although Helen seems curious about Jo's boyfriend, she does not seem especially interested in what he is like – and whether he is suitable for Jo. Instead she concentrates on how he might be able to provide them with free samples from the hospital. This offers us another instance of her irresponsible attitude towards motherhood.

As if to divert the conversation from her boyfriend, Jo asks Helen to look in the paper and see what is on at the cinema. One film advertisement catches Helen's attention, and her response to it brings out clearly several of the contradictions in her character. She says she finds it pornographic because it degrades women and presents them as sex objects. The highly moral pose she adopts in criticising the way men use women is reflected in the formality of her language. However, if we think back to her previous comments about men we see that she views men in exactly the same way that they view women; she judges them according to their sexuality. Then there is the way she presents herself to men. She might not be as blatant as the girl in the advertisement, but she relies just as much on her sexual charm.

This is followed by a further contradiction which although more comic, also amply demonstrates how her beliefs seem to exist only for the space of time it takes her to utter them. With the offending advertisement in front of her, she then jokingly wonders if she could turn Jo into a provocative sex symbol and put her into films. That is, do to Jo exactly what has been done to the girl in the advertisement.

The scene between them takes on a more serious tone when Jo suddenly asks on what day she was born. Such a question, and the one later about why Helen married, are doubtless prompted by Jo's own engagement. The casual cruelty of some of Helen's replies, and her abuse of her husband, offer a strong contrast to the attention that Jimmie lavished upon Jo, and show Helen's selfishness, clearly leading us to ask why Jo looks elsewhere for affection.

Once more, Jo introduces a new topic of conversation, as if to escape from the unpleasantness of Helen's attitude. But it offers only a momentary release because Helen stuns Jo with the announcement that she intends to marry Peter. The second half of Helen's speech leading up to this declaration is worth reading carefully because it once again shows how self-contradiction is at the heart of her character. The inconsistency of her ideas is all the more ironic when we consider the context of her words; she is giving Jo the benefit of her understanding of life. Helen suggests that we are not at the beck and call of fate, but can organize our own lives and decide for ourselves what we will do. This seems to be good advice, but her decision to marry Peter is obviously an ill-considered one and contradicts the good sense of her advice to Jo.

Jo's responses to this announcement need close study because they reveal a lot about her attitude toward Helen. First of all, her silence shows how deeply she resents the idea of her mother marrying. Then, when she speaks, the target of her blistering criticism is interesting because it helps us to understand her motive. It is not Peter's unsuitability as a husband that she mentions; it is Helen's age. Her reasons for doing this seem to be twofold. Firstly she wants to hurt Helen for betraying her by getting married; secondly by introducing the subject of age she is desperately trying to persuade her mother that she is too old to marry. In other words, we see once more Jo's ambiguous attitude toward Helen. She needs to hurt her, and yet she needs her. We feel as we read that Jo is frightened that if Helen marries she will be left alone. Her fear here contrasts with her confidence when she told Jimmie about leaving Helen and finding a room of her own somewhere. We are beginning to see with increasing frequency that beneath her brash exterior Jo is vulnerable and uncertain.

Pages 29–35

This section deals with the behaviour of Peter, Jo and Helen towards each other.

Look carefully at the four short speeches – two by Helen, one each by Peter and Jo – immediately after Peter enters because they are all revealing in their different ways. Helen's first comment could apply to the flowers and chocolates Peter is carrying. It is more likely, though, that it refers to Peter himself, for in her second speech Helen comments enthusiastically on how marvellous he is looking. What we see immediately about Helen in these speeches is how blatantly she shows that she is sexually attracted to Peter. She pays him far more attention than she ever does to Jo. Jo's comment is bitterly sarcastic, and seems designed to increase Peter's discomfort. Peter's own comment displays his lack of concern for and interest in Jo, despite the fact that he is soon to be her stepfather.

Jo's attempts to prevent the marriage take a variety of forms in what follows. The rude comments about her mother's figure are an obvious tactic to unsettle Peter, as is her cynicism about Helen's persistent lateness, the questioning of his reason for buying her chocolates, and the greedy way she eats them. When she is left alone with Peter she becomes more extreme, and shows us how close she is to total breakdown. Her anger, fear and jealousy spill over uncontrollably into hysteria as, half-laughing and half-crying, she attacks him, demanding that he leave her mother alone. Her desperation is more evident here than it has been anywhere else, making Helen's response crucial. We note that when Helen enters she immediately sides with Peter, and in doing so shows how thoughtlessly she puts her own chance of happiness before the welfare of her daughter.

Although the emphasis in this part of the section is on Jo's wish to prevent the marriage, we notice something else as well. If we look carefully at Helen's behaviour toward Peter we see that it is uniformly flattering: she compliments him on his looks, and later says he is marvellous to have found such a wonderful house for them. Peter's attitude towards Helen, though, is more mixed. He is not afraid to criticize her or to keep pictures of other women in his wallet.

Jo persists in trying indirectly to discourage him from marrying her mother. She makes a nuisance of herself and even resorts to sexual provocation. Although she does not succeed in tempting Peter, her behaviour reveals a development in her character. Jo is moving from girlhood into womanhood. She is becoming aware of her own sexuality and her own attractiveness. Contrast her behaviour here with the way she behaved with Jimmie earlier, and you will see that there is an element of conscious sexual teasing which was not present when she was with her boyfriend.

When Helen re-enters, Peter is genuinely delighted by her attractive appearance, but even so there is a darker undertone in his muttered comment about her having no sense of humour. We see, too, that it is only when Helen shows irritation with

Peter that Jo agrees to tidy her books away, as if she is seeking to emphasize for Helen the difference between her obedient daughter and her wilful boyfriend.

The titles of the books have their own significance, for they once more draw our attention to Jo's innocence, just as her fascination with Jimmie's toy car did earlier in the scene. Coming after her attempt to engage Peter's sexual interest in her, they serve to remind us how Jo is poised uncertainly between childhood and adulthood. And instead of being given help and guidance to understand what is happening to her, she is treated by her mother as if she is an unnecessary hindrance.

The extent to which Helen puts her own happiness before her duty to Jo can be seen in her willingness to leave Jo alone, perhaps for the weekend, while she goes off with Peter. Even though we credit Helen with honesty when she freely admits that she has never tried to be a proper mother, we find it hard to sympathize with her conduct here. Jo's mention of the job she starts on Saturday is an attempt to sound independent, but her bravado soon gives way to a touching, child-like fear of being left alone, and she asks if she can go with them. Helen's answer to this shows once again her lack of compassion for Jo and her eagerness to please Peter.

This section of Scene 2 has been the most sombre in tone of any so far. We have seen the desperate lengths to which Jo is prepared to go to prevent the marriage, from physically attacking Peter to trying to make him feel sexually uncomfortable. We also sense that the relationship between Helen and Peter will deteriorate, and that he will tire of her. Finally, we have seen Jo frightened of being left alone and pleading with Helen to take her, and then weeping on the bed in her solitary misery.

When we consider these points, we realize that Shelagh Delaney has not only presented us with some vivid drama as the three characters have clashed, but that the anger and bitterness, of the concluding part of the episode especially, provide a dramatically effective contrast with the gentler mood of the next section.

Pages 36–39

This section deals with the scene between Jo and Jimmie.

We notice immediately how the softer tone of this section is highlighted by the anger of the last one and so creates a mood which helps us understand why Jo decides to sleep with Jimmie. The transition between one episode and the next is cleverly achieved. There is music and Jo and Jimmie move towards each other as if dancing. The dreamlike effect of this sequence is enough to establish a new mood, and their dancing toward each other suggests harmony rather than discord.

Jo's denial that she has been crying, when in fact she has, shows her fear of being thought childish. Yet Jimmie's attitude toward her is anything but mocking. The concern he shows for her presents us with a noticeable contrast to Helen's selfish behaviour of a few moments ago. However, it is the influence of Helen, even though she is absent, which dominates the first half of the episode. Read it once more and you will see that this influence is both indirect and direct. It is there indirectly in Jo's response to Jimmie's comment that the children who live nearby are dirty. We feel that the attack upon their parents' neglectful attitude is also a veiled attack upon Helen. Then there is her assertion of her own uniqueness. In this Jo is like most teenagers who are anxious to be seen as individual in their own right rather than just as their parents' children. Even so, we feel that the comment has a special edge in Jo's case. It is as if she wants to disclaim any kinship or association with Helen.

Helen becomes the direct topic of conversation when we learn that Jimmie has passed her on her way out. Jo's attitude here is interesting, and quickens our sympathy for her, but Jimmie's attitude is equally interesting. Let's begin by looking at Jo. Jimmie's comments about Helen prompt Jo to ask if he fancies Helen and if he thinks she is beautiful. So Helen takes on another role in Jo's consciousness – that of sexual rival, and the scene underlines for us Jo's own sexual development.

As for Jimmie, we, like Jo, wonder if he is attracted to Helen. It is Helen, not Peter, that he first mentions as having seen, and although the way he speaks of her suggests that she is rather 'showy', it also suggests that she is rather alluring. When Jo later asks him if he fancies Helen, he does not give a straightforward answer. As you re-read this section of the scene, you will probably find it hard to make up your mind for certain one way or the other about the exact nature of Jimmie's feelings for Helen. But Shelagh Delaney has planted enough doubt in our minds to make us at least consider the possibility that he will not be true to Jo.

The topic of Helen then fades as Jo and Jimmie concentrate on each other. We notice that he compliments her on her pretty neck once more, and puts the ring on her finger himself. The effect of this tenderness on Jo, especially as she has just been abandoned for the weekend by Helen, becomes clear when she introduces the topic of Jimmie's wicked intentions toward her. Her youthful uncertainty is well presented in the way she is eager to give herself to him, yet frightened at first. As you read this passage, you might find that the references to Shakespeare's *Othello* intrude into the realism of the scene because they are too literary. Think about why Shelagh Delaney included them before you read the notes at the end of this Commentary, where there is a possible explanation.

Jo's invitation to Jimmie to spend Christmas with her is her way of inviting him to seduce her. Like so many important remarks in the play (Helen's announcement that she and Peter are to marry is another), it comes without advance warning, and we have to delve for possible reasons to explain it. Two are given here, although you might be able to think of others. The first is simply that she does not want to be alone. Jimmie, after all, has been attentive and loving toward her and this must seem a better alternative than a Christmas spent in a cheerless flat on her own.

The second is that her vision of her future has changed since she first appeared with Jimmie. Then she dreamed of marriage to him. Now she believes that she must not postpone her chance of happiness to some indefinite time in the future, but seize it while she can. (Compare her attitude here with that of Helen and you'll probably find it remarkably similar). She actually seduces Jimmie rather than letting him seduce her because she does not expect to see him again. Perhaps Jimmie's comments about Helen have revealed to Jo that he has a roving eye. Perhaps knowing that Peter keeps photographs of other girl-friends while engaged to Helen has made Jo suspect that men are unreliable.

Whatever the cause, she no longer has any illusions about Jimmie. We notice that she does not blame him, but seems to understand fully what his motives are. When he says that he loves her, instead of saying that she loves him also, she merely asks how he can say that when he has just confessed that all he wants is to sleep with her. This episode has seen an important development in Jo's character. Although she is still young and inexperienced, she now makes a deliberate choice to enjoy the present and disregard the consequences.

Pages 39–45

This section covers Jo's conversation with Helen on the day of her marriage to Peter.

Helen's excitement at the prospect of her marriage contrasts with Jo's cynicism. Just as she knows that once he has seduced her Jimmie will not return, so she refuses to be carried along by Helen's gaiety. At this point it is Helen who seems girlish and romantic and Jo who has a sardonic realism in her attitude to men. The discovery of the ring around Jo's neck makes Helen forget her self-absorption, and the dialogue between the two women up to the time when Jo asks about her father is worth reading carefully, especially for what it shows us of Helen's character. Her anger at Jo for getting engaged to a boy she scarcely knows is understandable, and shows that she is capable of showing concern for her daughter's welfare. As we read Helen's words of outrage, though, we feel that what she says to Jo applies equally well to herself, and so we have the irony of Helen, whose life is scarcely a good example for Jo to follow, dispensing the kind of advice she is incapable of following herself.

Helen herself seems to realize that she cannot lecture Jo in this way, and proceeds to offer herself as a bad example. Her tenderness here is genuine, but we note that Jo does not soften in her hostility, and this soon prompts more recrimination and anger from Helen. The way she swings rapidly from anger to affection and selfishness and back is not only a realistic portrayal of a quarrel between parent and child, but it also shows the complicated nature of Helen's relationship with Jo. Jo's behaviour toward Helen is more uniformly hostile in these exchanges than Helen's is to her, although we notice that she compliments Helen on her looks. Even though it is a double-edged compliment, it shows that amid all the acrimony, Jo can still display a reluctant admiration for her mother. We, too, find ourselves smiling at Helen's earthy humour

Jo's mention of her father broadens and deepens the play both in terms of its characters and its ideas. We can understand why Jo is anxious to learn about her father. As she grows older she naturally wishes to discover more about herself and wanting to know her father's identity is a part of this process. Helen's replies stun her. However, we note Helen's honesty here, and a little later when she confesses that she never thinks of the consequences of what she does. Of course, the knowledge that her father was rather stupid unsettles Jo instead of comforting her, and increases her self-doubt.

A closer look shows how the topic also influences the ideas in the play. Jo's disappointment in and disapproval of her mother have featured already and these emotions resurface here when she asks Helen how she could give her a father like that. Helen excuses herself by saying that she had no idea Jo would be the result of her brief affair. If we think ahead a moment, we realize that as she accuses her mother of thoughtlessness, Jo is already pregnant by Jimmie. Furthermore, the child she is carrying will be a half-caste. At the time the play was written, Brtitish society was far less tolerant of children of mixed parentage than it is now. So in her own way, Jo has been thoughtless too. Shelagh Delaney shows here how both women, wishing for a taste of honey, have lived for the moment. Daughter has been like mother, and in each case it is the child who stands to suffer most of all.

Strangely enough, Jo eventually begins to soften toward Helen, demanding to know the circumstances of the affair. Helen's reply draws our attention to her unhappy marriage, and reinforces one of the main ideas of the play – that happiness has to be grasped when and wherever possible. It is one of the few moments in the play when mother and daughter seem close. Jo comes as near as she can to expressing regret that Helen is going and even at this early stage Helen displays cynicism about the institution of marriage.

Naval rating Ordinary seaman.

Don't do that. You're always doing it Jo's comment here contrasts with the one she makes a little later when she says that she likes kissing him. Shelagh Delaney is showing us that although Jo is on the verge of womanhood, she is still not sure of how she should behave with a boy.

I don't know why I love you but I do The title of a popular song of the period.

I couldn't wear it for school anyway. I might lose it If the ring is too big, Jo might lose it whenever she wears it, not only at school. It seems likely that she mentions school because it is against the school rules to wear rings. This belies her claims of not caring, and shows how she is a curious mixture of dependence and independence.

when I leave school this week I start a part-time job in a bar Helen, we recall from Scene 1, started work in a bar. This offers another parallel between the two women.

Mau-Mau The name for the Kenyan movement for independence in the 1950s.

A siren is heard Sirens were commonly used to indicate the end of a shift in a factory.

I hope you exercised proper control over his nautical ardour Another of Helen's witty remarks which relies for its effect on a sophisticated vocabulary.

Has he got long legs? Helen has already expressed in Scene 1 her liking for men with long legs. Notice how she immediately concentrates on something which is of interest to herself.

national service A two year period of service in the armed forces to which men over eighteen were conscripted.

I was a Teenage . . . Some popular horror films of the time had titles such as *I was a Teenage Vampire and I was a Teenage Werewolf*.

The Ten Commandments An epic film released in 1958, the year the play was first presented on stage.

Desire Under the . . . Another popular film of 1958 was *Desire Under the Elms*, based on the stage play of the same title by the American playwright Eugene O'Neill. Notice the earthy joke Helen makes by leaving the title incomplete.

I agree with him . . . Still, why worry? These remarks of Jo and Helen show how differently they regard martial fidelity.

spiv A showily dressed man who lives on his wits. Rather like Peter, in fact.

There's two w's . . . no Arabian Knight A good example of the way Helen's speech often blends proverbial, traditional sayings with inventive wit. Here she puns on the popular Arabian stories entitled *The One Thousand and One Nights*.

Enter Peter . . . looking uncomfortable Peter's awkwardness as he enters shows us that he is not as suave as he tries to pretend.

here, Jo, have we got a vase, put these in some water Helen soon loses interest in the flowers. She wishes to focus all her attention on Peter.

I shan't be a tick I won't be long.

all the rest of the little bastards Peter's hostility toward his brothers and sisters helps to emphasize the difficulties of family relationships evident elsewhere in the play.

That's something about which I don't care to make a public statement Notice the change in Peter's tone here. He becomes more formal because Jo's questions irritate him.

'That wild destructive thing called love' A line from a popular song.

Why shouldn't I marry Helen? Peter does not answer Jo's question.

Perhaps he doesn't know why he is marrying her.

The art work takes a long time Jo is contrasting her own natural beauty with the efforts Helen has to make.

Bang-on Perfect.

Lord's Day Observance Society A group of people committed to keeping Sunday holy. Peter is sarcastically suggesting that Jo is being a killjoy.

He's got a wallet full of reasons Unlike Peter, Helen has a ready reason for wanting to marry, but it is hardly a very satisfactory one.

she can't live on grass and fresh air Another colloquial saying.

she's been called to the bar An example of Helen's humour. The term is generally used of barristers at the start of their career. Jo is to start work in the bar of a pub.

the black hole of Calcutta A dark cell in a prison in which 146 British prisoners were detained overnight in 1756. Next morning only twenty-three were found alive.

this is the dirtiest place I've seen Jimmie's comment echoes Peter's of a few moments ago, and emphasizes the social deprivation of the area.

the Pirate King Peter. Jimmie is referring to Peter's eye patch.

You've had your chips You're too late.

'gross clasps of the lascivious Moor . . . Oh Ill-starred wench' In Shakespeare's play, *Othello*, a Moor, marries Desdemona, a white girl. The play ends tragically. This might explain Shelagh Delaney's reason for including these references to it, for the affair between Jo and Jimmie ends unhappily.

down-and-out boozer knocking back the meths Penniless alcoholic drinking methylated spirit (a deadly form of cheap alcohol).

Old Nick Satan.

I'll like it in a few years when it isn't so new and clean Helen cheerfully admits here to being slatternly.

every line tells a dirty story There is a proverb which says 'every line tells a story' meaning wrinkles and marks on the skin show the kind of life one has led. Helen finds a wrinkle on her face and jokingly admits that the story it could tell of how she got it would be a dirty one.

I know Even though Helen knows what her weaknesses are she can do nothing to cure them.

Puritan Helen means that her husband disapproved of sex. Puritans were originally a very strict religious sect.

Questions and assignments on Act 1 Scene 2

1 Make a list of the similarities and differences in the way Peter treats Helen and the way Jimmie treats Jo. Here are some to get you started.

Similarities	Differences
both men enjoy touching the women	Peter is more openly sexual in the way he touches Helen

2 This scene broadens the scope of the relationships presented in the play. Write down what you learn about:

(a) Peter's attitude toward his family;
(b) Helen's attitude toward her first husband;
(c) Helen's attitude toward Jo's father;
(d) Jo's attitude toward Jimmie;
(e) Jimmie's attitude toward Helen.

3 Write an account of Jo's character based solely on the section of the scene which involves Peter.

4 Write an account of Jo's relationship with her mother, concentrating entirely on the last section of the scene (the one on Helen's wedding day).

Assignments

1 Describe an occasion when, like Jo, you felt alone and unhappy. What caused it? How did you cope with it?

2 Imagine that you are Peter and you have gone for a drink with some friends. What would you say about your relationship with Helen and Jo?

3 Compare the courtship of Jimmie and Jo with that of any two other young people you have read about in a book.

Act 2 Scene 1

As we can see from the stage directions at the beginning of the scene, it is now summer and Jo is obviously pregnant. But the directions tell us more than this. The noise, of the fairground, and Jo and Geof playing together, suggests happiness. This offers us quite a striking contrast with the first scene of the play where Helen and Jo began quarrelling as soon as they entered. The stage directions also draw our attention to the inconsistency between Jo's appearance and the way she behaves. Like a child, she is happy playing with a bunch of brightly coloured balloons, yet she is soon to have a child herself.

The relaxed and happy mood created by the stage directions continues when Jo and Geof begin speaking. Jo seems to be more self-assured, perhaps because she is no longer living in Helen's shadow. We notice that she has outgrown her fear of dark rooms, and this indicates a greater maturity on her part. She has become more self-centred as well. The last time we saw her with Jimmie, she had decided to seize her chance of momentary pleasure regardless of the consequences. This attitude has developed further in the intervening months. Although she needs her job to pay for the flat, she does not believe that she should slave away for anyone but herself.

As for Geof, his character quietly takes shape before us. He seems to be hesitant, and only enters the flat when Jo invites him in. Once there, like Jimmie in Act 1 Scene 2, he shows concern for Jo, sensing that she is hungry, and is willing to prepare food for her. Another similarity between Geof and Jimmie is their response to the flat. Both of them comment on the dirt and disorder. If we think about Geof's comment, however, we can see that it is significant in a way which Jimmie's was not. The squalour Jo lives in is entirely of her own making, for Helen is no longer there. It is easy for us to understand Jo's pride in having somewhere of her own, especially as she was so unhappy with her mother. But she no sooner expresses her proud independance than Geof's words show us that Jo's slatternly attitude to her home echoes that of Helen, the person she has said she most wishes to escape from.

So far, Jo has been the dominant figure in the relationship with Geof. This dominance continues when she asks him if his landlady has thrown him out. We see from some of her questions how perceptive she is; she senses that Geof is homeless, and then that he is a homosexual. His denial does not convince her, and her tone changes to one of curiosity and then to aggressive challenge, as she demands that he tell her about himself or get out. However, before looking at this, it is worthwhile considering the implications of Geof's homosexuality. So far in the scene, we have been struck by the similarities between Geof and Jimmie. Naturally, we begin to wonder if Geof's intentions towards Jo are going to duplicate Jimmie's. Jo's assertion that he is a homosexual cancels that possibility in our mind and we are curious to see if and how, their relationship will develop.

The dominance Jo has shown so far ends abruptly when Geof,

angry at her persistent questioning, prepares to leave. This moment reveals a great deal about both characters. His sensitivity to such enquiries is obvious. We sense how deeply hurt and angry he is. What is noticeable about J% is the suddenness of her capitulation. One moment she is laying down firm conditions – either he tells her or gets out – and the next she is pleading, quite desperately, for him to stay. Once more, Shelagh Delaney is drawing our attention to Jo's personal confusion. The self-assurance she has displayed in this scene so far is very fragile. Loneliness still frightens her, as it did in the previous scene.

Geof's observations about Jo's paintings invite us to recall what Helen had to say about them. His cool criticism of them contrasts with her enthusiasm; yet we accept his as the more valid view. Notice that he immediately sees how the style of the drawings reflects Jo's life; they lack shape and organization. His uncomplimentary remarks enrich his character for us. He might be gentle and sensitive, but he is perceptive, and prepared to criticize when he feels it is necessary. His comments also tell us something about what he values in life. He likes order and system, and in this respect is different from any other character in the play. In introducing Geof into the action, Shelagh Delaney has brought in someone who is reflective and serious. He will add another dimension to the types of relationship between people which the play examines.

The conversation which follows captures realistically the fluid nature of ordinary speech, and at the same time reveals further developments in Jo's character, defining more clearly for us the kind of relationship she will have with Geof. Consider the development of Jo's character: there are other characteristics worth noting, but three important ones emerge down to the point where Geof recites nursery rhymes. Firstly, Jo says that she does not know much about love. This makes us cast our minds back to her encounters with Jimmie and her attitude towards love then. This development from certainty on the subject of love to doubt shows how she is moving painfully toward maturity.

Secondly, Jo now buys make-up. Think back to the way she boasted to Peter about her natural beauty and you will see how she now regards herself as a woman rather than the kind of 'sweet young thing' Peter referred to. Think a little more carefully about that scene with Peter, and you will remember that Jo was drawing a comparison between her natural beauty and the artificial beauty of Helen. Her change in this respect emphasizes another similarity between herself and her mother.

Thirdly, Jo refuses to plan for the baby because it seems to be tempting fate. Of course, her refusal to look to the future has been part of her character since she let Jimmie seduce her. But we might feel that she has another reason for wondering if the baby will be born dead or retarded, and that is what Helen has told her of her own father. When we remember the profound shock that Jo felt on that occasion, it is easy for us to imagine her worry here over the welfare of her baby.

With regard to the relationship between Jo and Geof, his concern for her is quietly but genuinely expressed. Unlike Jimmie's, it is not accompanied by any wish to seduce her. We notice the positive pleasure he finds in planning for the arrival of the baby. We notice, too, how he gently tries to console Jo when she expresses fear for her baby's health. Almost intuitively, he brings her out of her moroseness, and the entire mood of the scene changes as they assert their own uniqueness. Once more, this reminds us of Jimmie's comment on his last appearance that he was one on his own, and Jo's reply. But there is laughter here with Geof which was absent on the other occasion. It is as though Geof has made Jo feel both secure and liberated.

As their gaiety gradually subsides, we notice once more the combination in Jo of the adult and the child as she comments cynically on free gift coupons and then promises to buy Geof a car. This element of make-believe in her character surfaces again when she describes Jimmie to Geof as a prince. She even has a romantic-sounding name for him. The anti-climax which comes when she then says that Jimmie is a male nurse in the navy is both comic and rather sad. Even though she knows the truth about him, she still needs to create a fictional identity for him which will satisfy her need for romance.

Her concern that Geof might not be comfortable sleeping on the couch is something which strikes us here. Such mutual care – his for her, and hers for him – occurs seldom in the play, and provides some of its most tender moments. Because she feels safe with Geof, she can even jokingly threaten to seduce him if he does not turn out the light. Her words at the close of the section are most important. She sees Geof not as a big brother, but as a big sister. In a sense this is true. Many of Geof's instincts are 'feminine' rather than 'masculine'. Whereas Jimmie was obviously looking forward to going for a drink with his friends in Act 1 Scene 2, Geof finds pleasure in domestic duties.

Pages 54–59

This section covers the action of the scene up to the entrance of Helen.

As we read through this section we realize that Shelagh Delaney is developing in more detail the relationship between Jo and Geof, and giving particular emphasis to the place sex has in it. The stage directions immediately highlight their differences in character. Jo wanders aimlessly about the room; Geof is purposefully engaged in making clothes for the baby. The tone of contentment which was there at the close of the previous section has given way to irritation. On Jo's part this is the result of the heat, although there is another, more deep-seated, cause. Looking through the door at a little boy she thinks is mentally retarded, she blames his mother for having him. We realize that what preoccupies Jo here is not the little boy's mother, but her own. She still blames Helen for giving her a retarded father. Obviously her anxiety that she, or her child, might be afflicted by some kind of hereditary madness has not lessened in the months since Helen told her.

The mood lightens briefly when she feels the baby kick. Geof's delight is especially noticeable. But this soon gives way to her taunting and sometimes cruel comments to him. We feel that her anger at Geof is really an expression of her own confusion. One moment she is sharing her pleasure with Geof; a little later she is being sarcastic about his domestication. Then later still she says that she feels like throwing herself in the river, as though Geof is in some mysterious way responsible for her unhappiness.

We notice that as the quarrel develops, Geof does not indulge her mood. He is critical rather than supportive, provoking Jo to make more cruel comments about his sexuality. If we read carefully, we see that this introduces a new aspect of their relationship. So far, they have lived as brother and sister – or as two sisters according to Jo. Now a sexual element appears which serves to make their relationship more complicated, and to show us how confused about themselves both Jo and Geof are.

It begins with Jo wickedly flirting with Geof. Her motives for doing so are complex. She obviously wants to hurt him and make him feel uncomfortable. But we sense that there is more to it than this. Jo has announced in the previous section that she hates love, and this might be true; but she cannot suppress her own developing sexuality. She is, after all, a young woman living under strange circumstances with a young man. Even though she is not sexually attracted to him, the temptation to try to provoke him sexually is great if only to prove something to herself, and she succumbs to that temptation here. This shows her own emotional confusion, and brings out an equally confused response in Geof.

He would like to be the father of her child, but of course he is not attracted to her as a woman. To complicate matters, in their relationship so far he has taken on what are traditionally seen to be feminine responsibilities such as cooking, cleaning the flat, and making baby clothes. He obviously finds satisfaction in this. But Jo's sexual teasing makes him wonder if she wants him to be more 'masculine'. He tries, but we notice the uncertain, tentative way in which he brings up the topic. He asks her what she would do if he started something; then he makes a clumsy attempt at kissing her. It is worth contrasting this with Jimmie's behaviour. Confident of his sexual identity, Jimmie desired Jo. Geof does not desire her in the same way and is here tormented by the conflict between what he actually is and what he thinks Jo wants. His attempt to make a pass at her is unsuccessful, but we note that Jo seems aware of the unhappiness she has caused by rejecting him and tries to placate him with chocolate.

But the matter does not rest there. The way Geof responds to Jo's remarks that it might be better if he left deserve close attention. He protests that he'd rather be dead and other equally extreme sentiments. Expressions like these might seem to us to be reminiscent of the kind of language used to voice romantic love, perhaps the kind of love which featured in the pop songs of the time. But we know that Geof does not really feel that kind of love for Jo, and so we wonder exactly what it is that he sees in her. You might have your own ideas about this, but it is clear that he likes caring for her, and that she will soon have a baby which he can look after. Jo herself is rather puzzled by the urgent and extreme tone of his words. In lying across the bed, she seems to be inviting him to define the nature of his regard for her. When he makes no move she knows what it is, and because he offers no sexual threat to her she agrees that he can stay. When we think about this scene between them, we wonder if she honestly wished him to go, for while she might not be physically attracted to Geof, she seems to be emotionally dependent upon him. Geof, though, is equally dependent upon her.

Pages 59–64

This covers the section involving Helen, Jo and Geof up to the time that Peter appears.

The section itself falls into two parts, the second part beginning where Geof leaves to make some tea. It might be worth our looking at them separately because the mood changes quite noticeably when Helen and Jo are left alone. Indeed, the mood changes when Helen comes in. Her breezy, sarcastic manner contrasts with the earnestness of the conversation which has been taking place between Jo and Geof. We notice how she immediately establishes her domination over Geof. We already feel that in any contest with Helen, Geof will be forced to yield.

What follows shows how disruptive Helen can be. As you read through this part of the section look at the confusion she generates which results in sudden and conflicting changes in allegiance. Helen begins by being assertive towards Jo. This attitude naturally makes Jo angry, and when she guesses that Geof has asked Helen to come, she turns her anger on him. Helen takes Geof's side, saying that Jo should not criticize him if she is living off him. This seems complicated enough, with mother taking the side of the 'boyfriend' against her daughter. But this lasts for seconds only, before Helen rudely tells Geof to shut up when he reminds her that Jo's baby will be Helen's grandchild. There are several similar changes of allegiance before the end of the scene.

Shelagh Delaney presents convincingly in this first part of the section the turmoil Helen creates. We see it in the increasing bitterness of the quarrel between Jo and Helen, as well as in the sudden shifts of allegiance. The quarrel begins with the women abusing each other verbally, but soon insults are accompanied by threats of physical violence, Helen upon Jo and Jo upon herself. We feel that the women feed upon each other's anger, and this in an odd way shows the closeness of their bond and their similarity as people. Helen almost admits as much when she tells Geof that they enjoy quarrelling. This is perhaps an over-simplification, but even so we wonder if they feel a strange sense of exhilaration as they try to out-insult each other. In all this, we see Geof helpless to restore order, and the limited influence he can have on either woman is clear to us. He even looks a little foolish when he yells for silence a split second after there is a lull. We notice that there is silence not because he demands it, but because for the moment the quarrel has worn itself out.

The furious pace of the action here might distract us from three other points which we should consider. Firstly, there are Helen's remarks that local people disapprove of Jo. So far in the play, the scope of the action has been limited mostly to what the main characters think of each other. Now we are given a glimpse of what ordinary outsiders make of it all. Although Jo has disregarded conventional morality, she is judged morally by her neighbours, who regard her actions in a less than sympathetic light. Of course, it is ironic that Helen should be the one to comment on this because this leads us to wonder what the same neighbours think of her behaviour with Peter.

The second point involves Geof and Helen, and their relationships with Jo. In many respects, Geof has fulfilled the function of mother during the past months. Now, Shelagh Delaney has introduced Jo's real mother, and they occupy the stage together. Helen's fury and verbal cruelty provide an ironic contrast with Geof's gentle concern for Jo's welfare.

Thirdly, several of Helen's remarks draw our attention once more to the contradictory nature of her character. Look at the number of times she states that she has no responsibility for Jo. It might strike you as odd that Helen is saying all this while she has accepted some sort of responsibility for her by doing as Geof asked and coming to visit. In other words, if she truly did not care then she would not have come. And the genuineness of her concern becomes evident in the second part of the section, when Geof makes the tea and the women are left alone.

Even though Jo is still aggressive, the mood here is much softer, and that is because Helen refuses to be provoked. Look carefully in this sequence at the offensive and sarcastic remarks Jo makes, and look equally carefully at the moderation of Helen's replies. The scene between them is one that we can easily relate to as Helen wants to make amends and Jo wants to continue the quarrel. We can probably all remember occasions when we behaved as Jo and Helen do here. The measure of Helen's involvement with Jo, whether she wishes it or not, is her comment that she has been unable to sleep for thinking about Jo. As you read this scene between them, you will probably find it difficult to side with one or the other of the characters. Jo's accusations, though true, are cruel; Helen's desire to help her daughter, though genuine, is likely to be inconsistent. The difficulty we have in deciding where our sympathies lie is part of the play's strength. We feel that it refuses to give any easy answers, preferring instead to present us with some of the awkward ambiguities and conflicts which are part of family relationships.

Pages 64–69

This section covers the action of the play from the time Peter comes in until the scene ends.

The Peter who enters now cuts a very different figure from the one who appeared earlier. Every vestige of sophisticated worldliness has gone. He is the worse for drink, and takes as much savage pleasure in hurting Helen as he previously took delight in flattering her. Obviously, their relationship has soured beyond repair. If his drunkenness is one sign of his deterioration, his vulgar sexual remarks are another. When we first saw him in Act 1 Scene 1, he brought with him an openly sexually suggestive manner, but he did not resort to the kind of obvious crudeness which is such a feature of his speech in this scene. We wonder what Geof must make of what is going on.

However, as we read, we come to realize that there is a kind of manic comedy in much of what Peter says. He seems in some respects to be like a stage drunk, behaving in an exaggerated disorderly manner, not just making crude remarks, but falling helplessly around the stage. We feel that like many drunks, he finds his own behaviour amusing, even if no one else does, as he insults in turn the other three characters.

His jokes can be rather less crude than this, though, and even more hurtful. The Oedipus story he tells Geof is an example of this. In fact, Shelagh Delaney uses this story, and Helen's reaction to it, to jolt our memory very effectively into recalling their earlier attitude towards each other, and how that attitude has altered. We remember that when Helen told him she was old enough to be his mother, he caressed her and told her he rather liked the kind of mother/son relationship they had. It was his way of complimenting her by saying that he liked older women. Now he has changed. (A little later he even boasts that he left Helen for a fortnight and had an affair with a younger woman). He uses the myth of Oedipus to emphasize what is for him the sordid nature of his relationship with Helen, an older woman.

Helen's response is interesting. Of course, she understands the point of the story, and realizes that it is meant to hurt her. But she doesn't seem to be annoyed by the fact that it is a veiled attack upon her. What does annoy her is that for her it is a dirty story — one of many which Peter seems to know. When we remember the intimate delight she took in the dirty story he told her in Act 1 Scene 1, we can see how disillusioned she has become with him, and also how much she has changed.

Further evidence of this change is apparent when Peter lurches off-stage to be sick in the lavatory and Helen asks Geof to look after him. For a moment mother and daughter seem almost friendly but the moment soon passses, after which Jo once more becomes hostile. As in the previous section, though, when Geof had left them to make some tea, Helen refuses to be provoked. Clumsily, perhaps, but genuinely, she expresses concern with Jo's appearance, and then invites Jo to live with her. Jo's response, especially when she has laid such store by her independence from Helen, is predictable. But this does not alter our feeling that Helen has perhaps belatedly come to accept the responsibility she has for Jo. How long she will maintain such an attitude is more difficult to say. We might also wonder if she would show such responsibility if her life with Peter was still harmonious and exciting.

The dilemma Helen faces is highlighted for us in the action which takes place from the time Peter re-enters. We notice that Helen puts to the test her place in her relationship with Peter when she states before him that her home is Jo's. For this, she receives only sarcasm from Jo and flat contradiction from Peter. Faced with Peter's announcement that he is leaving, Helen must decide whether to go or stay. Shelagh Delaney catches very well Helen's struggle between duty to her daughter and dependence upon a husband who, by his own admission, hates her. It is a humiliating moment for Helen as she weakens and finally goes.

Running as an undercurrent throughout the final section of this scene has been the contrast between the relationship of Helen and Peter and that of Jo and Geof. The marriage of the former is clearly unsatisfactory. We have to look more closely for evidence of the way in which Jo and Geof treat each other, but there are examples here which show that even though they quarrel bitterly with each other, they are capable of tenderness as well and there are examples of this throughout the scene.

If you think back to Jo's behaviour earlier when Helen left with Peter to go to Blackpool, you will notice the contrast here. Then Jo was distraught; now, with Geof, she has a measure of security.

maisonette A flat, usually on two floors.

straight on up the creek Straight into trouble.

under the arches Homeless people sometimes sleep under the arches of bridges.

people like you Jo believes Geof to be a homosexual.

You want taking in hand You want someone to look after you. As it becomes clear a little later, Geof is offering to look after Jo himself.

I'm not having everybody staring at me Contrast Jo's sensitivity here with the brashness of her comment to Jimmie in Act 1 Scene 2 when she said that she didn't care if people saw them together. The two comments show the difference between Jo, as she would like others to see her – rebellious and self-assured – and a more unsure, tentative young person.

Spratts A firm which made dog biscuits.

I like them Geof's liking of nursery rhymes is something he shares with Jo and it draws the two of them closer together.

Lagonda An expensive Italian sports car.

school Art college.

I'll stay here and clean this place up a bit . . . You're just like a big sister to me Remarks like these do rather more than indicate what Geof is like. They show how his relationship with Jo can work to their mutual benefit. If, as Geof said earlier, she needs someone to look after her, then he just as surely finds great satisfaction in being the one who does it.

walking away Jo means that the little boy has lice in his hair.

Nobody asked you to stay here. You moved in on me In her anger, Jo has forgotten that she pleaded with Geof to stay.

Someone's got to look after you. You can't look after yourself Geof's motives for staying are not quite as selfless as he suggests. He has his own reasons for staying with Jo, prominent among which are the pleasure he finds in domestic duties, and his eager anticipation of the birth of Jo's child.

croft A dialect word for a piece of waste ground.

You're going to need me after Contrast the certainty of Geof's tone of voice here with his more hesitant words just a little later when Jo turns to him, he to her. Instead of telling her she needs him, he asks if she does, and so displays his own fear that she might reject him.

Romeo A slang name for a lover, after Shakespeare's *Romeo and Juliet*.

you put years on me You make me feel old and bored.

Victorian melodrama Melodrama, with its stereotyped characters such as the villian, the pure maiden, and the gallant hero, was popular in Victorian times. Helen's purpose here is to insult Geof by assigning him a very subordinate and, for a man, inappropriate role – nursemaid.

set-up Arrangement.

When I'm talking to the organ grinder . . . to answer Musicians playing portable organs in the street were once quite common. They often had pet monkeys which begged money from passers-by. Helen is suggesting that the relationship between Geof and Jo is similar to that between an organ-grinder and his monkey. That is, that Geof is somehow in charge. Yet seconds earlier she had scathingly referred to Geof as the nursemaid. The inconsistency of remarks like these help to capture the realistic tone of the quarrel. Helen is more concerned with establishing her dominence over Geof and Jo than with being consistent.

When the cat's away Part of a proverb. When the cat's away, the mice will play. Helen means that Jo took the opportunity of misbehaving with Jimmie when she was away with Peter.

Sling your hook! Get out!

Can you cut the bread on it yet? A semi-crude colloquial remark. Helen wants to see how big Jo's belly is.

pansified Effeminate.

I thought it was the tea-break I thought there was a truce in the quarrel. Jo is being sarcastic because she feels Helen is still nagging her.

maternity benefit An allowance given by the government to expectant mothers.

You're nothing to me Jo's words to Helen are identical to her words earlier to Geof. In both cases we feel that they are gross over-simplifications of the way she feels towards them.

'Little Josephine, you're a big girl now' Peter is not so much referring to that fact that Jo has grown up, but crudely joking about her pregnant appearance.

Temperance Society A national movement which warned about the dangers of drink. Helen is being sarcastic.

bun in the oven Slang for being pregnant.

Lana The first occasion when Peter insultingly calls Geof by a girl's name.

'Getting to know you' The title of a song from a musical called *The King and I*.

Oedipus In Greek legend, Oedipus was fated to kill his father and, unknowingly, marry his mother, Jocasta.

Well, is anybody coming for a few drinks?   It is only because he is drunk and therefore incapable of understanding the effect he is having that Peter could ask such a question.

He picked up a couple of grapefruit ...   Peter speaks in a leering tone of the young woman with whom he had an affair.

fruitcake   Slang for homosexual.

I was out   I didn't have any left.

Questions and assignments on Act 2 Scene 1

1   Make a list of the most important aspects of Geof's character which emerge in the first section of this scene. (Up to the point where he leaves the stage carrying the bedclothes.)

2   Now read the second section of the scene (up to Helen's entrance) and add any new features of Geof's character which you feel develop here.

3   Write a brief account (three or four paragraphs) showing how Geof and Jo behave towards each other in these two sections.

4   Re-read the section with Helen, Jo and Geof and say what you find convincing or unconvincing about the argument they have.

5   Explain briefly, in two paragraphs or so, how Peter brings an element of coarseness into the final section of the scene. Look at:

(a)   the way he speaks to and of Jo;
(b)   the way he speaks to and of Helen;
(c)   the way he speaks to and of Geof.

Assignments

1   Imagine that you are Geof. Write an account of your feelings towards Helen from what you have noticed about her in this scene.

2   Contrast the relationship between Geof and Jo with any other relationship between two young people in a book you have read (for example, that of Gregory and Dorothy in *Gregory's Girl*).

3   Write an account of a quarrel you have either witnessed or been involved in. You can present it in dialogue form if you wish. Try to bring out the anger and the cruelty of which people are capable when they quarrel.

Act 2 Scene 2

Pages 69–76

This section deals with the scene up to the arrival of Helen.

As we learn from the stage directions at the beginning, this scene takes place some months after the previous one, and Jo's baby is due soon. By now we have become used to the characters dancing on and off stage to music, thus helping to create a dreamlike atmosphere which exists alongside the realism of the dialogue and the presentation of character. As if to emphasize the distinction between real life and art, we are told that 'in reality' months have passed between this scene and the previous one. This reminds us of the 'unreality' of the events by focusing our attention on the selective nature of what we are shown. Real life is one continuous, fluid process, often with no obvious shape or pattern to it. In this play, as in all plays, we are only being given significant glimpses of the lives and relationships of characters.

When we begin reading this section we see how the time between this scene and the last has altered and consolidated the relationship of Jo and Geof. What strikes us immediately is their happiness together. As in any relationship, this is not a constant factor, but it is nevertheless a genuine one. It is evident in Jo's teasing of Geof at the beginning of the section. When we think back to the cruel way she teased him sexually in the previous scene, we are made more acutely aware of the difference here. Time has brought them closer together. In the intervening months, Jo's advancing pregnancy has banished flirtatious thoughts from her mind. This has had a liberating effect upon Geof. Whereas in the previous scene he felt he had to prove himself sexually to her, now he is happy caring for her, confident that Jo will not ridicule his lack of manliness.

In fact, it is the change in Jo which is most marked. Settled into a reassuring and comfortable routine, she has blossomed. Our attention is drawn, through her home-made housecoat, to the gradual development of a domestic side of her character. Equally significant perhaps, is that Geof feels able to joke about how badly it is made, confident that she will not respond in a touchy, offended manner. In this happy state she is able to take pride in her pregnancy, something which she acknowledges is due to Geof's influence upon her. This, too, is a new facet of Jo's character. Up to now, she has been reluctant to admit that she depends on anyone. Even when speaking well of Geof she has never said anything more than that she liked him. Now, more confident of herself, she is better able to appreciate him.

The buoyant mood of the opening gives way to a more reflective sequence arising out of Geof's discovery of Jo's bulbs under the sofa. We observe that it is Jo who changes, not Geof. In fact, the constancy with which he is presented serves as a dramatic contrast to Jo's sudden changes of mood. It is an effective piece of drama, for it serves to enrich Jo's character by showing us that she is a rounded, complex personality capable of spontaneous joy and unsettling reflection.

The dead bulbs lead her to ponder on life and death, and especially the seemingly casual way in which we are called into being. She sees life as being chaotic, having no shape and no purpose. Her thoughts are presented as general observations, but it is clear to us that she is speaking of her own position. Herself the result of a casual liaison between her mother and a virtual stranger, she too is carrying a child by a man she scarcely knew. In the midst of her happiness with Geof, this sombre thought on the way she was thrust into existence and is doing the same to her child frightens her. We note that Geof leaves his housework to comfort her, as presumably he has done many times before. The contrast between Geof and Helen in this respect is made explicit by Jo's comment that Helen never let Jo hold her hands.

Then Geof draws Jo's attention to the similarity between her and Helen, and Jo's reaction to his words is worth nothing. She pushes his hand away and teases him, a little more cruelly than she did at the start of the scene. But only a little more. What we notice is the almost total absence of anger. It is not that she is pleased to be compared to her mother; it is that her regard for Geof is such that she will accept from him remarks that would arouse her fury coming from anyone else.

The mood becomes exuberant once more when Geof makes her laugh, but as was the case earlier in the scene, laughter and jokes give way to more anxious reflection as Jo speaks of her father. It is hard to over-emphasize the effect Helen's cofession has had upon Jo. It surfaces here again in what is at once a criticism of Helen and an unspoken admission of fears for her own, and her baby's, sanity. Running counter to this is Geof's brisk dismissal of what Helen has said. A little earlier we saw him offering Jo comfort by taking her hand and speaking soothing words. Now a different, more reasoned form of reassurance is required; instead of petting here, he needs to give a level-headed, sensible dismissal of Helen's claim. He does this and Jo is soon laughing.

As we read Geof's words, though, we might find that we too are convinced by what he says. His argument that it is unlikely (though not impossible) that Helen would go out with someone who is retarded casts a new doubt, at least in our minds. Even though Jo seems unaware of the possibilities we are left to ponder whether Helen told Jo the truth or was, instead, being incalculably cruel to her daughter by suggesting such a thing.

Helen, although absent, seems to loom large, like an oppressive shadow, over the relationship between Geof and Jo. So far in this section we have seen Jo's preoccupation with her mother surface both indirectly (when she commented on the haphazard way life comes into being) and directly (when she spoke of Helen's unwillingness to hold her hand, and here when she speaks of Helen's affair with her father). And this preoccupation culminates in Jo's wish that her mother was with her now that the birth of her baby is close. This admission is extremely important, for it shows that despite everything Helen has done to her, Jo's ingrained need for her mother overrides every rebellious and individualistic sentiment she has voiced.

The incident with the doll shows how volatile Jo can be. Her sudden violence, so out of keeping with the mood in the section so far, makes us realize that beneath the precious stability that Geof has given her there runs a deep current of panic. The nature of this panic is complex, and compellingly presented by Shelagh Delaney. When you read the speech in which Jo loses her temper, you will notice that like all the speeches in the play it is short. Shelagh Delaney does not tease out for us the implications that lie behind what Jo says; she leaves us to do that for ourselves. Let's look at what some of these implications are.

For one thing the colour of the doll (it is white) reminds Jo forcefully of the mixed race of the baby she is carrying. Whereas she had earlier seen her affair with Jimmie in a romantic glow, implicit in her words here is her painful realization that her child will be born into a society which is not liberal in its attitude towards such children. But this is only part of the reason for her outburst: equally important is that Jo does not want to be a mother at all. Scarcely more than a child herself she is soon to be forced into the role of mother. It is not only the responsibility which frightens her; it is that by virtue of having given birth she will be a woman, a grown-up, required to take on a new identity without ever having had the chance to savour for herself the delights of childhood. Her earlier remarks about freedom, independence, and setting up on her own have a hollow ring of naivety to them when set against the cruel lesson which experience has taught her.

We notice once more how Geof gradually restores her equilibrium, even drawing from her Jimmie's real name. This in itself marks a significant step in her growth to maturity, for she now discards any pretence of romantic illusion. It is ominous that as they laugh together, and share in the duties of making tea Helen comes in, laden with baggage.

Pages 76–79

This section deals with the scene between Geof, Helen and Jo up until the time that Geof leaves.

The settled, though delicate, environment that Jo and Geof have created for each other is fractured by the arrival of Helen. Look at her first two speeches and you will see by their length and their energy that she dominates from the moment she enters. Words tumble from her lips; questions are asked without answers being expected, disapproval expressed at Jo having the baby at home, and Geof is first ignored and then insulted. When we consider the care Geof has taken of Jo, Helen's audacity here is such that neither of them seems to question her motives for coming at all. She grandly announces that she has come to look after Jo. But in her first speech she remarked that it was a lovely day for 'flitting' – or running away, for the truth is that she has left Peter. She is, therefore, homeless. We are left to wonder how much her sudden arrival is a question of convenience for herself, as she has nowhere else to go, and how much concern for Jo. She has certainly left it to the last minute to offer advice and support to her daughter!

Geof's gentleness, which has been such a valuable quality in his care of Jo, becomes a handicap when matched against Helen's abrasive vigour. He capitulates quickly. One of the things we must consider in this section is whether he capitulates *too* quickly. The argument in favour of this view is that, within not more than a couple of minutes of Helen's arrival, Geof is offering to move out. However, various aspects of the scene suggest that it is Helen's forcefulness rather than Geof's weakness which brings about the final outcome. Although he eventually leaves on the pretext that they need groceries for the weekend, it is quite clear that Geof knows Helen has won the battle of wills between them, and his part in Jo's life is over. He has seen her in action before when she had a furious row with Jo, so he knows that her behaviour here is not exceptional; also Helen's calculatedly cruel remarks to him would make living in the same flat difficult for someone as uncertain of his sexual identity as Geof is. Jo's words urging him to stay are inevitable but also inevitably unsuccessful.

Even she cannot cope with the disorder Helen trails in her wake, by turns being angry with Helen for criticizing Geof and then impatiently criticizing him herself.

Pages 79–81

This section deals with the dialogue between Jo and Helen until Geof returns.

The exchanges between Jo and Helen in this section represent an important development in their relationship because although they bicker with each other, they never become abusive or insulting. We begin to sense an inevitability about their coming together again. Notice the way in which Helen brushes aside Jo's instructions that she must not be rude to Geof by denying that she ever has been. She pushes the subject of Geof to the periphery of the conversation, not even answering Jo when she asks her to leave him alone, but talking about baby clothes instead. Yet Helen is more on the defensive in this section than she was in the previous one. We observe that she parries Jo's question about whether Peter has thrown her out by introducing the topic of Jimmie. However, both women know each other too well by this stage of their relationship to be deceived for long. Helen knows that Jo's claim that she can do anything she wants to is adolescent wishful thinking. Jo for her part knows that Peter has abandoned Helen, and Helen herself finally admits this.

Shelagh Delaney's portrayal of Helen is very interesting here. For one thing, there is her automatic assumption that she can step in and resume her life with Jo as if nothing has happened – as if she had never married Peter and Jo had never met Geof. The failure of her marriage seems to have caused her hardly any distress. It is rather as though she had married Peter hoping for the best but expecting the worst. Yet it is not quite as simple as that, for Jo is convinced that Helen still loves Peter. Jo's insight into people has frequently struck us with its acuteness, and so Helen's strenuous denial does not necessarily convince us. We might even feel that Helen's resilience on this occasion is not merely the product of natural exuberance, but is something consciously striven for.

It might be, then, that Helen is coping with being hurt. It is perhaps because Jo understands the pain of being abandoned by a man herself that she does not take the opportunity to gloat, but rather comments that she and Helen are back where they started. In one sense this is true, but experience has changed them subtly. Helen honestly confesses that when she was happy with Peter she never thought of Jo, but Jo's own pregnancy gives her the strength to accept this without bitterness. For the first time in her life she has a role to fulfil, and her developing maturity is apparent in her belief that she could take care of the whole world including Helen.

The sentiment is reciprocated, for Helen shows a wish to care for Jo. She has ordered a cot for the baby. She tells Jo to have a lie down and – significantly – Jo does as her mother bids. By the end of this section, as Helen sets about tidying up the flat (another development in her character), we begin to feel that Geof has been set aside. Jo, of course, expresses her loyalty to him by saying that she likes the wicker basket, but we have already become aware that the strongest bond in her life is still with her mother.

Pages 82–84

This section covers the action of the scene up to the time that Geof finally departs.

Whereas the previous section showed Helen in a softer, caring mood with Jo, this one brings out all her antagonism towards Geof. She shows this quite clearly in the unrelenting way she criticizes and belittles him. Virtually everything she says to him is designed to increase his discomfort and make him feel unwelcome. From this point of view it is an impressive performance, against which Geof is unable to retaliate. Helen's skill in seizing the initiative is all the more impressive when we consider the actual weakness of her case. Her sudden fixation with cleanliness sits ill with her slovenly attitude earlier in the play. Her contemptuous remarks about the food he has bought sweep aside his lame, though true, comment that Jo likes the basket and this kind of food.

Yet through sheer dynamism Helen defeats him. We note how, in contrast to Geof, Helen shows little interest in what Jo actually wants and is far more concerned with what she thinks Jo ought to have. Helen's fixed ideas on what proper food actually is, her determination that the baby will sleep in a cot, and her horror when Geof mentions that Jo wants him with her when she has the baby, show not so much her love for Jo as her determination to have her own way. The contrast between the two of them is finely dramatized by Shelagh Delaney, Geof showing by his unselfishness how much he cares for Jo; Helen showing by her wish to organize Jo how narrow her idea of caring actually is.

The struggle between them, which has so far been verbal, is presented in visual terms when Geof empties the food onto the table. It is the most assertive gesture he has made in this part of the play. Even here, though, Helen dominates, thrusting it back at him and finally throwing it all on the floor. The episode demonstrates for us, and for Geof, Helen's physical (as well as her verbal) dominance. With the bitterest words he has uttered at all he leaves.

Pages 84–87

The final section covers the action from the departure of Geof to the close of the play.

There are three sharply differing moods in this section. The first, until Helen goes to the kitchen, is characterized by its extreme tenderness. When Jo wakes, Helen is soft and reassuring, in total contrast to her brusque manner with Geof a little while ago. It is no accident that her first words to Jo are reminiscent of those parents use to soothe frightened children, for

Shelagh Delaney is showing Helen here as being everything that a caring mother should be. It is possible that she is heeding Geof's plea not to frighten Jo, for she makes light of the pain of childbirth, and stops Jo thinking morbid thoughts.

We might begin to wonder if Helen has come genuinely, if belatedly, to motherhood. However, even in the midst of this rather idealized picture of mother and daughter, Shelagh Delaney has given us cause to doubt the possibility of its continuing. Helen lies to Jo about Geof. And such an idyllic relationship built upon a lie cannot last when the truth is known. Furthermore, when Jo's labour pains start, Helen feels the need for a drink. The pains pass, and Helen regains her composure, but her reliance upon drink makes us wonder how much help she is going to be to Jo when she begins to give birth. We might even recall her words to Jo earlier in the scene when she confessed that she could not stand trouble.

The trouble comes in the second phase of the section where the mood is one of panic rather than of love and gentle reminiscence. All Helen can do in response to Jo's announcement that her baby will be black is to make two impractical suggestions – that it should be drowned, and that perhaps the midwife (who is black) will adopt it – before she leaves Jo once more, this time to get a drink. Yet as we read the closing pages we notice that, although she is overcome by the news, she does not become abusive to Jo as we feel she once would have done. What could be a moment of dramatic climax is punctured as she makes a direct appeal to the audience. Furthermore, there is a strain of frantic comedy running through the whole sequence, as she asks Jo where her hat is, only to be told it's on her head, and rushes out.

The final words rest with Jo, however, and the mood softens once more. Although Helen has told her she will return, we can hardly be sure of this. Jo, however, can face this possibility. She looks to the future smiling, and in her closing song pays an indirect tribute to Geof, who did so much to help her come to terms with herself and with her pregnancy.

'Ninth month' Note the subtle and natural way we are told that the birth of the child is imminent. Jo is reading from the book that Geof bought her.

Little Women A book for girls by the nineteenth-century American writer Louisa May Alcott. Its tone is very wholesome, and Jo is using it to mock the style of the book she is reading which coyly calls a baby 'a little stranger'.

book barrow A stall selling second-hand books.

Edwardian . . . Ted The reign of King Edward VII from 1901 to 1910 is known as Edwardian. At the time the play was written, in the mid-fifties, many young men adopted and exaggerated certain features of Edwardian fashion. They became known as Teddy boys or Teds. Jo is gently mocking Geof here. The drainpipe trousers, velvet-collared jackets and violent reputation of the Teddy boys is far removed from Geof.

What's in the oven Geoffrey? . . . You what? Jo's abrupt transition from the subject of her pregnancy to asking what's in the oven confuses Geof for a moment. Remember Peter's vulgar song 'Who's got a bun in the oven?'

Haven't you shifted the sofa since then? Bulbs are placed out of the light in order to help them germinate.

'And he took up his bed and walked' Jesus miraculously healed a cripple. Jo is making a joking reference to the fact that Geof is pushing the couch – his bed – back into position.

Now you're being Irish Now you're not making any sense at all.

Ibsen's *Ghosts* A play written in 1881 by Henrik Ibsen in which one of the characters, Oswald, is going mad. Geof's point is that Helen has an over-active imagination.

spin me a yarn Tell me a story.

She likes to make an effect. Like me? Another way in which Jo resembles her mother.

Scoutmaster Tales of scoutmasters who make improper advances to scouts have become part of popular mythology. The important point here is that Jo feels secure enough of Geof's response to actually make such a joke to him.

Oh, Jo, I'm daft at times . . . There, look, isn't it good? Read Geof's words carefully here and you will see how tentative he is about giving Jo the doll, almost as if he suspects what her reaction will be.

Helen enters loaded with baggage, as in Act 1 Scene 1 An important stage direction for it shows how circular Helen's life is. Any attempt to break the pattern inevitably fails and she returns to where she started.

I'll tell you one thing, it's a lovely day for flitting A wonderful example of Helen's natural resilience. From the gaiety of her tone here one would never guess that she is admitting that her marriage has failed.

Flying Doctor The name of a popular television drama series in the 50s. Set in Australia, it was about a group of doctors who flew to outlying ranches to deal with medical emergencies.

like a bull in china shop In a clumsy, awkward manner. Notice how Jo's comment draws our attention to the physical presence which Helen establishes. It is not just that she dominates the conversation;

her assertive physical movements underline her vocal assumption of power. We can imagine that Geoff would find such 'barging around' not at all to his taste.

swanking Boasting.

What does the little lady want – an engagement ring? Jo is mockingly reminding Helen of Peter's words in Act 1 Scene 1.

throw-back An ape-like creature.

He threw his money about like a man with no arms Peter was mean.

etceteras It is a de-luxe model.

Mrs Smith, I . . . I . . . Notice Geof's hesitant manner as he broaches this sensitive topic, and how this hesitancy continues into his next two speeches. Helen's impatience with him provides an obvious contrast.

She can't cope with the two of us Geof is right, of course, but his reason for leaving seems to be largely because he is unable to cope with Helen.

Clough A ravine or steep valley.

If you don't like it you can get out. I didn't ask you to come here Jo's words here are uncannily similar to those she uses to Geof in Act 2 Scene 1. However, where she was incorrect then, she is correct here. We feel that even if Helen does leave, Jo will cope.

Questions and assignments on Act 2 Scene 2

1 The first part of this scene (up until Helen arrives) is built upon a series of comic or light-hearted moments followed by more reflective or sombre ones. Make a summary of each one so that the pattern becomes clear.

2 Write three or four paragraphs suggesting how and why Helen is different in the second part of the scene (when she first appears) from the way she behaves in the third part (when she is alone with Jo).

3 Make a list of the criticisms Helen makes of Geof in the section where he finally leaves.

4 Show how Helen and Geof have different attitudes to Jo in this section.

Assignments

1 Compare the relationship between Jo and Helen in the final section of the Scene with that of any other mother and daughter you have read about in a book.

2 When Helen appears, Jo seems to feel her loyalties divided between Geof and her mother. Write about an occasion when you felt divided loyalties.

Shelagh Delaney's Art in *A Taste of Honey*
The characters

Jo

I don't want to be a mother. I don't want to be a woman.

Jo is the most important character in the play. Except for a few brief periods – when she makes the coffee for Helen and Peter in Act 1 Scene 1, and when she lies down in Act 2 Scene 2 leaving Helen and Geof alone – she is on stage the entire time. Of all the characters, she is the one we come to know in most detail, as we see her progress towards maturity.

Although her relationship with Jimmie has profound consequences for her, because it leaves her pregnant, it is Helen's influence which is the most enduring. It is because of Helen's negligence as a mother that Jo is so confused about herself, and this confusion leads her to behave in two seemingly contradictory ways; she can be both vulnerable and yet self-assertive. In fact, when we read the play closely we realize that they are not contradictory at all; she is aggressive precisely because she feels so unsure of herself. Being at an important but difficult stage of development in her life – no longer a child, not yet an adult – does not help either. Although Jo's case is extreme, it will be helpful if you consider how convincing a portrait she is of someone who is at this awkward stage of growing up.

Most of the time with Helen she behaves as though she is completely sure of herself. This is largely because, in the perpetual battle of personality that she has with her mother, to express any uncertainty would be a sign of weakness which Helen would exploit. You will have noticed how Jo never misses an opportunity to score points off her mother. There are examples throughout the play, but a glance at the first page only will show you that she criticizes the flat her mother has found, Helen's immorality, her forgetfulness, and her laziness. In order to survive alongside such a dominating personality as Helen, Jo not only belittles her mother at every opportunity, but praises herself whenever she can. You might feel that such boasting on Jo's part is not so much a sign of confidence as evidence of a lack of it.

We begin to see her vulnerability a little more clearly when Peter enters. She makes her dislike of him very clear, but does not take the chance to get out of his company by taking her bath. Instead she makes some coffee and pointedly sits down to watch him with Helen. Her purpose in doing this is made clear when Helen remarks that Jo is jealous of her (Helen) being affectionate with anyone. What this means is that Jo sees Peter as a rival for her mother's attention. In other words, despite her constant rudeness to her mother, we begin to see that Jo needs her more than she realizes; otherwise she would not care about Helen's affair with Peter.

When we read her first scene with Jimmie, we see that Shelagh Delaney further establishes Jo's self-assertion (she says that she doesn't care what people think of her) and her immaturity (her interest in Jimmie's toy car). To this she adds Jo's desperate need to be loved, a need which Jimmie seems to fill. The attention he pays her — waiting outside school for her, carrying her books, and so on — is in deliberate contrast to the way in which Helen ignores her. For the first time in her life Jo feels cherished, feels that she can enjoy a taste of honey, and automatically assumes that she is in love.

We can see the extent of her personal confusion in her second meeting with Peter. She begins by being aggressive to him, but her worldly cynicism soon crumbles. Like an hysterical child she attacks him, demanding that he leave her mother alone. Her reason for hating him is clear here — he threatens her relationship with Helen. But then a little later she changes towards him again and begins flirting with him. We notice that she is sexually provocative here in a way she was not with Jimmie. In this episode we can see that Jo does not behave as a child who sees Peter as a rival for Helen, but as a woman who is engaged in a kind of sexual rivalry with her own mother. This marks an important development in her character. It is not that she finds Peter attractive. It is that she is growing up and becoming aware of her sexual identity. We feel that this growth towards physical maturity lies uneasily alongside other aspects of her character. The titles of her books, for instance, suggest a need to lose herself in the fairy-tale world of children's fiction.

The next section, her last with Jimmie, shows a further advance in her character. Between Jo's first scene with Jimmie and this one she has lost her romantic glow. From being excited about a happy future together, she now accepts that she will probably never see him again, and is content to take whatever pleasure she can when it is offered. She offers no reason for this, although as we suggested in the Commentary it is perhaps because seeing photographs of Peter's other girlfiends has convinced her that men are unreliable. In any case, it shows Jo becoming a hardened realist in a world which will offer her little security. The similarity between Jo and her mother here is obvious.

One of the aspects of her character which might strike us as most convincing is that these developments towards maturity are not presented as a smooth progression. Jo sometimes appears to be growing up and coming to terms with herself, only to show how frightened she is a little later. It is in this way that Shelagh Delaney shows us what a painful and inconsistent process growing up can be. Look, for example, at the section where Jo and Jimmie are together in the flat, and contrast it with the next section where Helen tells Jo about her father. Jo is sure of what she wants, takes the initiative with Jimmie, and seems to understand him better than he understands himself. With her mother, though, she reveals deep-seated uncertainty about herself (she wonders whether she is mad) and about Helen's feelings towards her.

In Act 2, we see the same process slowly continuing. Jo is proud of her independence and is happy to work all day in a shoe shop and all night in a bar to pay for the flat. Yet she pleads with Geof not to leave her. He provides the emotional support she has lacked so far in her life. When we read Act 2 Scene 1, we notice that this is not easily achieved. At first they seem happy together as Geof sings songs to her and she promises laughingly to buy him two Lagondas. She admits that she feels safe with Geof because she is sure that he will not start anything. Yet as the months go by Jo seems to find herself confused by the brother/sister relationship she has with Geof. We notice that she flirts with him, but when he tries to respond she pushes him away saying that she dislikes all this panting and grunting. We notice also the first signs of her resentment towards her unborn baby.

By Act 2 Scene 2 her relationship with Geof seems to have settled into a reassuring pattern for her, and Jo is at her most contented. We sense that this is partly because Geof asks nothing of her, leaving her space to come to terms with herself. She has become more domesticated, even making herself a housecoat. She and Geof often speak to each other in a teasing tone which shows their affection for each other. It is noticeable that Jo is less aggressive now because she no longer feels unwanted.

She is still vulnerable, though, and prone to anxiety about her father's sanity, and to very real resentment against her baby. In fact, her attitude towards her unborn child is significant in that it shows a conflict between her maternal pride and her knowledge that she has been made to grow up before her time. However, the end of the play shows Jo beginning to resolve this conflict also. Being alone no longer frightens her. We notice that although she is now close to giving birth, Jo does not panic at Helen's sudden departure. Her time with Geof has given her the opportunity to mature in a caring environment. She acknowledges her debt to him in the final words of the play (a song he had sung to her) and in her tender memories of him. As a result of knowing Geof, Jo is now more secure in her independence. She is not aggressive or assertive, but quiet and reflective. By the close of the play we have come to see that she can face the future not with the romantic dreams she had of a life with Jimmie, nor even the rather cynical attitude she displayed when she invited him to stay with her. These have been replaced by a quiet self-confidence that she will be able to cope with whatever the future holds for her.

Question and assignments

In what ways would you say that Jo is both similar to and different from Helen? It might be helpful to consult and add to the notes you made in answer to question 4 after the Commentary on Act 1 Scene 1 (page 17).

Assignments

1 Imagine that you are Peter. Write a brief description of your feelings for Jo.

2 Jo decides to write to Geof at the art college to thank him for what he has done for her. What do you think she would say?

3 Make a list of the ways in which you think Jo changes during the play.

4 Imagine that you're Jo. Write about how your feelings for Jimmie change as the play progresses.

Helen

The extent of my credulity always depends on the extent of my alcoholic intake.

As one of the two most important characters in the play, Helen needs close study. She strikes us immediately as being a believable character. This realism is due partly to her speech and partly to the fact that, like most of us, she is often inconsistent in her behaviour. This last point is an important one; her habit of contradicting herself, of saying one thing and doing another, is a strength not a weakness in the presentation of her as a character because she emerges as a fully rounded human being.

Let's look at what these characteristics are. Firstly, it has probably occurred to you that she displays a great range of emotional behaviour; she can, for instance, be both caring and extremely cruel, and these are features we might recognize in our own personality. The following examples of each will show you the extremes of which she is capable. She is impressed by Jo's drawings and offers to pay for her to go to art school. Later in the play, she tells Jo that she has been unable to sleep for worrying about Jo's pregnancy. By contrast, she can be bitingly cruel, as we see from her remarks that Jo should turn herself into a bloody termite and crawl into the wall, and later her assertion that her daughter is like a little bloodsucker living off Geoff. What we notice, though, is that these are extremes. Helen is not someone who is naturally vicious, nor is she someone who is particularly caring: sometimes her conscience is pricked and she worries about Jo; sometimes Jo upsets her or gets in the way and Helen is cruel to her.

Mostly, however, Helen is concerned with herself and her own pleasure, and this is the second important characteristic she displays. You will find examples littered throughout the play. For instance, when Peter enters in Act 1 Scene 1, we notice that Helen soon loses interest in Jo. And she puts her own chance of enjoyment before her duty to her daughter when she leaves Jo alone over Christmas. Remember that it is during this period that Jo invites Jimmie to stay with her and becomes pregnant as a consequence. These are two important examples, but even seemingly minor details show how this characteristic is deeply ingrained in Helen.

Helen's love of pleasure is the kind which enjoys the moment without giving any real thought to the future, and we can see her irresponsibility as another important feature – the third – of her character. Her life has consisted of a series of fleeting tastes of honey. Each of them has brought her momentary pleasure, but each has left her afterwards no better off than when she started. The two most important examples in the play are her affair with Jo's father – a five minute affair – which not only ruined her marriage but left her with a daughter she did not want; and her marriage to the obviously unsuitable Peter.

Her life has little shape or pattern to it as she drifts from flat to flat, from affair to affair. Yet while setting Jo no good example herself, she sometimes gives her advice on how to live her life, and this leads to the fourth important element in Helen's character – the inconsistency between what she says and what she does. It is worth looking closely at two examples of this. The first is the 'work or want' speech in Act 1 Scene 2 which was mentioned in the Scene Commentaries. Helen's idea that we are in control of our destiny is contradicted not only by what she says in the latter half of the speech, but by the way she lives her life; she is driven by her desires rather than by her reason. The second example comes later in the same scene when she discovers that Jo is engaged. As a parent, her anger at Jo is quite understandable in the circumstances. But Helen's comments that Jo is useless, that it takes her all her time to look after herself and that she is a stupid little devil apply as justly to the mother as to her daughter. From what we have seen of Helen we know that she is hardly likely to be an efficient, supportive wife to Peter, even if he were a suitable husband.

This suggests a fifth ingredient of her character for we might see this lack of self-awareness as evidence of a kind of immaturity in Helen. In some respects she is more like a child than Jo is, eager for instant gratification with little regard for the consequences. Look, for example, at the way she heaps flattery on Peter in Act 1 Scene 2, and flaunts herself sexually in front of him. Even more immature is her behaviour a little later in the scene when she enters with fancy boxes containing her wedding clothes. She is too carried away by the romance of it all to consider the consequences of what she is doing. Her childish enthusiasm is made all the more noticeably by Jo's cynical comments.

We can see Helen, then, as unrealiable, selfish, irresponsible, at the mercy of her desires, and often immature. By any standards she is an appalling mother. She offers Jo no secure home base and little or no emotional support, let alone love. We notice that when she returns to care for Jo her motives for doing so seem mixed: she has left Peter and has nowhere to go. Furthermore she soon gets rid of Geof, the only person who has cared consistently for Jo. And when Jo is close to giving birth Helen forgets all her tender words about caring for her daughter, and rushes out for a drink to help her cope with the shock of learning that the father was black. Given all this, we might wonder why we don't condemn Helen completely. In fact it is hard to do this, you might even find her rather likeable.

One reason for this is that, despite all her faults, Helen is often disarmingly honest about herself and her attitude towards Jo. She admits in Act Scene 1 that she supervised her own downfall, and blames no one but herself. And she does not even pretend that Jo comes first in her life. Helen openly admits in Act 1 Scene 2 that she has never claimed to be a proper mother, and you might remember that in Act 2 Scene 2 she confesses to Jo that when she has been happy she has never again given her daughter a moment's thought.

Another reason for our sympathy is the hint we are given of her unhappy childhood – you might recall that in Act 1 Scene 1 Helen says that she would not have dared to speak to her mother the way Jo speaks to her for fear of being beaten. We also have knowledge of her unhappy first marriage.

Two other points affect the way we see her. Firstly, Helen is often very funny. Her remarks when she reads out the film titles in Act 1 Scene 2, for example make us smile, and this helps to soften the way we see her. Finally, Helen shows great resilience. Life has not been especially kind to her, but she has not become embittered as a consequence. She hopes for happiness with Peter, but does not seem particularly surprised when the marriage fails. Look at the occasion in Act 2 Scene 2 when Jo says that she believes her mother still loves Peter. Helen's protestation might strike you as not entirely convincing, but she knows that the marriage is over, that it was good while it lasted, and that there is no more to be said.

Questions and assignment

1 Using the details given in the play, write a brief biography of Helen up to the time the play opens.

2 Make a list of the reasons why you think Helen is such an important character in the play. Here are some to get you started:

(a) Helen presents an important contrast with Geof;
(b) Helen helps clarify Jo's character.

3 Write a paragraph outlining Helen's attitude to marriage.

Assignment

Write a description of Helen as you think Peter might see her.

Geof

I'd sooner be dead than away from you

Geof gives Jo more consistent care and attention than anyone else in the play, even Helen. He does this partly because he finds deep personal satisfaction in looking after her, and partly because he has a more fully developed sense of responsibility than any of the other characters. This sense of responsibility enables him to plan for the future in a serious way – such as making practical preparations for the arrival of Jo's baby. You will have probably noticed that this makes him very different from either Jimmie or Peter. He is different in another way also. Unlike them, he is thoroughly domesticated, enjoying what have been traditionally considered to be feminine roles – cleaning, sewing, cooking.

Apart from the fact that he is an art student, we know no more about his background than we know of that of Jimmie or Peter. We do not even know for sure whether he is homosexual or not. When Jo raises the matter early in Act 2 Scene 1, Geof is unwilling to speak about it, and we notice how easily hurt he is. Sensitivity is one of his most prominent characteristics (contrast Peter), enabling him to understand Jo's fears and to try to offer emotional support. Look at the way he cheers her up in Act 2 Scene 1, for instance, when Jo says that she is making no plans for the baby in case it is still-born or retarded, and again in Act 2

Scene 2 when he holds Jo's hand to comfort her in her fear. The emotional security Geof provides for Jo cannot be overestimated because it weighs so heavily against Helen's failure in this area. The security he offers her contrasts strikingly with the fleeting sexual pleasure (or taste of honey) which Jimmie gave.

Despite his gentleness however Geof does not let Jo have her own way in everything. You will have noticed that early in their relationship he is about to leave when she persistently questions him about his sexuality; it is Jo who begs him to stay. A little later he has some very unflattering things to say about her drawings. Nor does he always indulge her mood. When they have been living together for a month or two and Jo is tetchy because of the heat, he speaks sharply to her, even telling her to stop pitying herself.

It is shortly after this that Jo, rather cruelly, begins to flirt with him, and the question of Geof's sexual identity is raised again in our minds. He is clearly rather 'feminine' in many of his characteristics, but this is not to say that he is actually a homosexual. He seems to be in some doubt about his own sexuality, and Jo's flirtatiousness brings about a crisis in him. He seems to think that she wants him to adopt a more traditionally masculine role with her. Look at the way he asks Jo what she would do if he started something, and his clumsy attempt to kiss her, and you will see how unsure he is of himself in this kind of role. It would be hard to imagine Jimmie behaving in such a hesitant manner.

If Geof gives a great deal to the relationship, he also benefits a great deal. Because of his sexual confusion, he requires a relationship which asks nothing of him sexually but which allows him to express the tender and caring side of his nature. In Jo he meets someone who is almost perfect for him, for she needs emotional stability and non-sexual love. The fact that she is pregnant is a bonus for him, allowing for still further fulfilment, in the future when he will not only have Jo to look after, but a child as well. He is rather like a mother looking after her pregnant daughter.

It is his sense of responsibility that makes him tell Helen of Jo's pregnancy, although he must question the wisdom of having done so when she arrives and is abusive to him. He cannot assert himself against her, and we see for the first time that the gentleness which has been so beneficial to Jo will make him a victim of Helen's relentless energy. This does not happen immediately, for the scene he and Jo share at the beginning of Act 2 Scene 2 shows the many different sides of their relationship before Helen enters once more to destroy it. We notice how they joke with each other and tease each other (Jo even teases him about his possible homosexuality without making him angry or embarrassed). When Jo mentions Helen's story about her father, Geof is quick to give her sensible reasons for not believing it. More tangibly, he has made a cake for tea. One of the last pictures we have of them alone together is of Geof carrying the cake and Jo carrying the tea things — both of them finding pleasure in sharing a domestic duty. Then Helen enters.

Geof simply does not have the force of personality to cope with her. When you read the scene where he and Helen are alone (when Jo is lying down) you might feel that although Geof has justice on his side, Helen has sheer force. He realizes that his presence will now be harmful to Jo if he stays, as there will be continual conflict between Helen and himself. When you read this scene, and think about Geof's decision to go, remember how deeply committed he is to Jo and her baby. He said earlier (in Act 2 Scene 1) that he would rather be dead than away from Jo. Unlike Peter and Jimmie he is not given to making grand statements which cannot be relied upon. His departure is made at great cost to himself, and is the most unselfish action in the entire play.

Questions and assignment

1 Write down these two headings and then give at least three examples of each from the play.

Practical Support *Emotional*
for Jo *Support for Jo*

2 Write a character study of Geof

(a) as Jo would see him;
(b) as Helen would see him.

Assignment

Imagine that you are Geof. Explain why the relationship with Jo was so important to you.

Peter

The world is littered with women I've rejected.

Peter is the least likeable of the three male characters in the play. As with Jimmie we learn very little about his background. He is a car salesman, has plenty of money, does not seem to like his family much, and has only one eye. He tells Jo that he lost the other in the war, which may or may not be true. However, even from these brief details we learn something about how Shelagh Delaney sees him. For example, car salesmen have a reputation for being plausible but unreliable, and these are certainly two of Peter's characteristics. His eye-patch gives him a certain swaggering, debonair quality, but also makes him look like a stereotyped, rather comic villain – Jimmie laughingly refers to him as the Pirate King. So even from the little background detail we have, it is possible to see Peter as someone who likes to cut a dash in the world, but who is not as urbane and sophisticated as he likes to imagine.

His behaviour in the play bears this out. In his first scene we notice that he is not only sexually attracted to Helen, but actually tries to seduce her in front of Jo. From the start, then, we see how careless he is of Jo's feelings when they conflict with his own desires. But when you read this section of Act 1 Scene 1, you should pay particular attention to the way he attempts to seduce Helen, because it shows him up as a vulgar man trying to be sophisticated. His openly sexual attitude towards her – his petting of her, and his suggestive comments, for instance – together with his dirty jokes show him to be uncouth. Yet he sometimes tries to give the impression of being suave and wordly by making witty or coolly self-possessed remarks – for example, when he tells Helen that she knows she's glad to see him, and calls her 'kid,' a term used by tough-guy actors in Hollywood films. It is obvious, however, that he is not very successful in presenting this image. Even Helen makes fun of the enormous cigar he is smoking.

One point you must think about is why Peter is so deeply attracted to Helen, at the beginning of the play at least, when she is several years older than he is. No clear reason is given, and you might have your own views. However the possibility that Peter feels that being seen with an older woman – especially a beautiful older woman – adds to his own lustre is worth considering. So his interest in Helen can be viewed as another aspect of the selfishness he has shown in his attitude to Jo. As for his proposal to Helen, which sits uncomfortably with his wish to present himself as a denonair man-about-town, it implies that although he likes to give the impression of being in control of his life, he is in fact a creature of whim and impulse unable to think seriously about the future, and already taking refuge in drink. You might find him rather similar to Helen in this respect.

On his second appearance most of these characteristics re-emerge and are developed. We notice how he strives to make an impressive entrance bearing flowers and chocolates, but only succeeds in looking uncomfortable. It is a grand gesture which falls flat. We notice, too, how his attempts at being a ladies' man (see his remarks to Helen about his appearance) are once again unconvincing; for example, his comment to Jo to stop 'guzzling' the chocolates is hardly very debonair!

His selfishness becomes more apparent in this scene. We notice the two occasions when he expresses impatience with Helen for not being ready and for having no sense of humour, and feel that the marriage is hardly likely to be successful. His behaviour towards Jo is just as important. Remember that he is about to become her step-father, yet he makes no attempt to understand why she should feel resentful of him, and shows very plainly his dislike of her. His view of his own family is obviously important here. He does not feel close to them, and his unhappy background affects his relationship with other people.

The third time we see him, the worst aspects of his character are given free rein. Every vestige of sophisticated behaviour has gone. Rather than seeing himself and expecting to be seen as a success he is obviously a failure; he has failed in his marriage, he has failed with his family, and he had failed with Jo. We feel that his boast about his affair is pathetic rather than glamorous. All he can do is stumble round in a drunken stupor being offensive to Helen, Jo and Geof.

Peter not only offers an important contrast to both Jimmie and Geof he also helps develop the characters of Jo and Helen. Like Jimmie he clearly enjoys sex, but is more vulgar, cruel and less sure of himself. He is different from Geof in being a womaniser who perhaps needs sexual conquests to boost his own self-confidence. His presence in the play also reveals Helen's attitudes towards marriage and money while at the same time helping to show us how confused Jo's attitude is towards her mother; she professes to hate Helen yet she sees Peter as a rival for her mother's attention.

Questions and assignment

1 Can you suggest reasons other than the ones given why Peter wished to marry Helen?

2 Make a list, from Peter's point of view, of what has gone wrong with his marriage to Helen.

3 Write down what you consider to be the main aspects of Peter's character, and give an example for each one. Like this:

Womaniser	photographs in wallet
Insensitive	tries to seduce Helen
	in front of Jo

Assignment

Write an essay about how you feel toward Peter. Do you feel sorry for him or not?

Jimmie

I will come back, I love you.

When you first read the play, you might have found yourself asking questions like these: Does Jimmie really love Jo? Does he become engaged simply because he thinks she will then go to bed with him? Is he wrong to abandon her? Is he rather like a younger version of Peter? Are his tenderness and concern for Jo all part of a scheme to disguise his dishonourable intentions? To try to sort out what kind of person he is, let's gather together the facts of his character, and then look at the way he behaves.

One of the most noticeable things we discover when we start listing the facts is how few of them there are. In other words, we do not know much about Jimmie; neither does Jo. This is not because he tries to conceal what he is, but because she is not interested in what he is really like, only in what she imagines him to be. However, we know that he is black, a naval rating, aged twenty-two, that he was born in Cardiff, and was a male nurse before he joined the navy. Two important points emerge here – his colour and his occupation. We wonder if perhaps these are two fundamental reasons why Jo is attracted to him. By having a black boyfriend (very uncommon in the 1950s) who is also a sailor (remember the reputation as womanisers that sailors have), Jo is possibly trying to shock, and so draw attention to herself. In other words, if we believe that Jimmie has an ulterior motive in going out with her, then she has one in going out with him, and so it is difficult to blame either one of them for what happens.

Of course, Jo is not callously using him and neither is he callously using her. She actually likes being in his company, and if you put yourself in her position for a moment, then it is easy to see why. Jimmie is very attentive to her; he waits outside her school and carries her books home. He seems to cherish her; he tells her he adores her and even kisses her hand lovingly when he puts the engagement ring on her finger. He likes being with her; he wishes he was not in the navy so that he could spend more time with her. And he makes her laugh; the way he proposes to her prompts her to accept in a joking manner. There is no reason to believe that this is all part of some carefully laid plan to seduce Jo into sleeping with him. Like Jo, he is young and like her, he finds the idea of being in love very appealing. When he speaks of love and marriage he probably means everything he says, at the time he says it. However, when the circumstances of his life change and he rejoins his ship, we can imagine that Jo then becomes just a pleasant memory. Jimmie is not nasty or sly, like Peter, but he is not especially reliable either. You might have met people like him yourself.

There is another point in his favour. He makes no secret of his wish to sleep with Jo. In fact, she is rather flattered by his attempt to seduce her on the deserted football pitch. And having been foiled on that occasion, he neither deserts her nor puts her under further pressure to sleep with him. You might feel that his proposal of marriage is a way of encouraging her to sleep with him. If so, then you have a point. However, there is nothing in the play to suggest that he is using it as a means of winning her over.

In fact, it is not so much Jimmie who seduces Jo as Jo who seduces Jimmie. It is she who invites him to stay with her over

Christmas. You will notice in their final scene together that he is concerned that she has a cold, and he is generally very tender to her. Just as important in this scene is his honesty. He makes no attempt to hide the fact that his intentions towards Jo are dishonourable, and he tells her that he thinks Helen is beautiful. The only occasion when he possibly evades a question is when Jo asks him if he fancies Helen, but even this does not matter to Jo. She has decided that she does not love him; she simply wants his company over Christmas. You might have noticed that there is no reason for Jimmie to say that he loves her, or to promise to come back to her, for Jo has already offered herself to him and told him that she expects nothing in return. He says it because he believes it. It is only when he has left her that he discovers he did not mean it. Jo knows him better than he knows himself.

Although Jimmie appears in only two scenes, his influence in the play is crucial. Think of the way that he affects not only Jo's life, but Geof's and Helen's as well. His presence also deepens the significance of the title, for Jo provides him with his own taste of honey; he seems to find pleasure in the idea of being in love with her, but she provides him with a sexual triumph as well. The confidence he has in his own sexual identity is in marked contrast to Geof's own uncertainty about himself. Finally, the freshness of his relationship with Jo emphasizes the sordid nature of the affair Peter is having with Helen, as well as providing a further contrast with the non-sexual relationship between Jo and Geof.

Questions and assignment

1 Make a list of the points against Jimmie which you think Helen would make.

2 Make a list of points in Jimmie's favour which you think Jo would make.

Assignment

Using the points you have made, write a scene in which Jo and Helen argue about Jimmie.

Location, setting and place

Location

Location is obviously very important in *A Taste of Honey*, and at first sight there seems to be no problem: the play is set very firmly in Salford, Lancashire. Shelagh Delaney tells us as much after the cast of actors has been listed and even before the play has started. But if we think about the matter for a moment or two, we might see that the location is not quite as straightforward as it seems to be. We have already noticed that on several occasions our attention is drawn to the unreality of what is happening. Characters address the audience, dance, sing, and make their entrances to music. Are we meant to assume, then, that when people in Salford approach each other they dance, or when they come through a door music strikes up? Obviously not. Shelagh Delaney uses such devices to remind us that what we are seeing (or reading) is a play, not a documentary, or even a work of art which is masquerading as a slice of real life. The characters seem real, of course, as does the kind of language they speak, but they have no existence outside the theatre.

In this respect, the character of Helen, for example, simply ceases to be when she is offstage and we cannot see her. So although the play is supposed to be taking place in Salford, it is in fact taking place on stage: any stage, anywhere. It might be helpful, then, if we use the terms 'setting' and 'place' to distinguish between these two locations. The play is set in Salford; it takes place in a theatre.

If you find this so obvious as to be not worth stating then you have a point, except that by breaking the illusion of reality, by drawing our attention to the fact that it is a piece of theatre, Shelagh Delaney herself is making us aware of it. Think of plays or episodes of series that you have seen on the television. They have a setting – London's East End, or New York, for instance – although many of the scenes might have been shot in a studio miles away. However, because the actors do not break the illusion of reality we accept that the setting and place are one and the same. If we see a location shot of a street in London's

East End and then the inside of a cafe we accept that that is where the cafe is situated (even though it might only be part of a television studio) and that the identity of the characters in the cafe is real, and we are watching a slice of life. However, if the characters in the cafe started talking to us, or dancing towards each other we would have to revise our opinion and see them not as real people but as performers, and the whole play as a performance. That is precisely what we have to do with *A Taste of Honey*. It is by bringing together a realistic and recognizable setting (Salford) with a theatrical sense of place and occasion that Shelagh Delaney has given the play one of its most distinctive qualities.

Let's now look separately at setting and place.

Setting

The Salford in which Shelagh Delaney has set her play is a place of slum dwellings and dirty, uncared-for children. You must use your imagination to create a picture of the flat and its surroundings if you are to appreciate the squalor in which Jo and Helen exist, for their lives, and their hunger for a taste of honey, must be viewed against this social deprivation in order to be fully understood.

As you read the play, you will become aware that although Shelagh Delaney focuses her attention on the flat, she provides unobtrusive yet necessary detail of the area in which it is situated as well as tiny but telling glimpses of the people who live there. If we take the flat first, we notice how quickly its bareness and lack of comfort are established. It has a shared bathroom, old and stained wallpaper, a leaking roof, inadequate heating, and, perhaps most depressing of all, an unshaded light bulb. As if to remind us of its dilapidated condition, Shelagh Delaney strews references to it throughout the play: Peter (Act 1, Scene 1), Jimmie (Act 1 Scene 2), Geof and Helen (Act 2 Scene 1), and Helen again (Act 2 Scene 2) all comment on the dirty, uncomfortable place. The fact that Jo and Geof can find a degree of happiness together in such a place is an indication of the power of human beings to resign themselves to the unpleasantness of their surroundings and even rise above them. It is almost as though they can put up with them because they expect nothing better.

The setting of the play is further enriched by the way in which Shelagh Delaney creates a geographical and a social context for the flat. That is, we see the flat as part of the area in which it is situated, and we are given an insight into the lives of the people, especially the children, who live there. The flat is a slum dwelling in a slum area distinguished by its ugliness. It is near the gasworks, the slaughterhouse, a foul-smelling river, a 'croft' or patch of rough ground, and a cemetery. Peter, Jo, Helen and Jimmie all comment on the awfulness of the area. The people who live there are socially deprived. Jimmie remarks in Act 1 Scene 2 on the filthy children he has passed, and in Act 2 Scene 1, Jo comments on one particular child who is severely neglected. She does so while the children are singing in the street, and the happiness of the children as they play is contrasted effectively with the squalid surroundings. Although Shelagh Delaney is not writing a play of social protest, by using detail like this she shows us the blighted opportunities of these children and, of course, of Jo's child which will be born into such an environment.

Place

Even though the play is set very firmly and realistically in a part of Salford, as we saw above, it often draws our attention to its own artificiality and reminds us that it is taking place in a theatre. This technique is popular in some modern drama and originated in the work of a German playwright named Bertolt Brecht (1898–1956). In order to break the stage illusion, Brecht had his characters address the audience and comment on the action of the play. He called this an 'alienation device'. Its purpose is to stop members of the audience from being swept up in the action – to 'alienate' them from close emotional identification with the characters – and encourage them to view more objectively the social and political implications of what is taking place onstage.

As we mentioned above, *A Taste of Honey* is not really a social or political play, but the Brechtian device of alienation is still apparent. When you read through the play, you might find yourself identifying with the characters, trying to understand them 'from the inside'. No sooner have you done so than you find this identification being interrupted by characters actually speaking to you or dancing on or off stage to musical accompaniment. And so you might find yourself having to step back from the action and consider exactly where you stand in relation to what is going on, rather than immersing yourself uncritically in the action and letting it wash over you. The alienation effect is perhaps more apparent when the play is performed than when it is read, but you should still try to picture what is happening in the stage directions as well as in the dialogue because this will help you appreciate the flavour of the play. In Joan Littlewood's production in 1958, for example, the characters came and went to the accompaniment of individual signature tunes played by the band. This drew attention to the fact that they were performers or entertainers, rather in the way that many television celebrities are instantly recognizable by a few bars of music which are associated with them.

If you read the play more carefully still, you will see that there are not so many of these alienation devices in Act 2 Scene 2, and for long stretches the theatrical illusion is complete. We might actually be in a flat in Salford, and we can participate imaginatively in the relationships between Jo, Geof and Helen. When Helen enters and Geof leaves, returns and leaves again they do so without dancing on and off stage, and without music. Yet the end of the play once more draws our attention to its theatricality. Helen leaves with a question to the audience: what would they do in her position? Jo sings a song which reminds her of Geof. Nothing has been finally resolved. We don't know if Helen is coming back, even though she says she is; and we don't know how well Jo will cope with her baby when it actually comes, even though she is serene when we last see her.

In the film version of the play, these alienation devices were abandoned in favour of a more consistently realistic approach. For example, we see Jo at school, and working in a shoe shop. We are shown in detail how she becomes involved with Jimmie, and how she first meets Geof. The effect destroys the delicate dream-like atmosphere of the stage-play where things merely seem to happen without any need for detailed explanation.

Questions and assignment

1 Make a list of Peter's remarks about the flat, and the area in

which it is situated. Then write two or three paragraphs showing what this tells you about him.

2 Contrast Helen's attitude toward the flat in Act 1 Scene 1 with her attitude in Act 2 Scene 2. What does this tell you about the way she has changed?

Asssignment

Imagine that you are writing part of the film version of the play. Two of the scenes will include Jo talking to her schoolfriends about her future with Jimmie, and Jimmie talking in a pub to his friends about Jo. The scenes will come before they spend Christmas together. Write *one* of these scenes, setting your work out as a script for acting.

Time

Under this heading we will look firstly at the way Shelagh Delaney deals with the idea of time in the play, and then consider briefly how the time in which it was written – the 1950s – affects the kind of play it is.

You probably discovered in your reading of the play that little attempt is made to give the reader a detailed notion of how much time is passing. The problem is even more acute when the play is performed because the audience do not have the stage directions to tell them that several months have passed between, say, Act 2 Scene 1 and Act 2 Scene 2. This is another instance of Brecht's alienation technique mentioned in Location, where one scene seems to flow easily into another without any close or consistent regard for time. In fact, if you think about it, there seem to be two time scales operating in the play, one that bears some resemblance to reality – the nine month period of Jo's pregnancy – and another that seems to be a purely theatrical notion of time which we aren't meant to question too cloesly.

The real time-scale in the play is fairly easy to follow. It seems to cover a time-span of just under twelve months, say ten or eleven. Within this framework, 'theatrical time' operates with great flexibility and helps to create the distinctive atmosphere of the play. It does this by lying alongside the 'real time' and together they produce a curious effect of reality and artificiality in much the same way that the realism of the characters lies alongside the artificiality of their dancing and addressing the audience. It's worth thinking carefully about this because the real/unreal atmosphere of *A Taste of Honey* is one of its most noticeable features, and it is not there in the film version should you see it.

Some examples will make this clear to you. When we first see Jo and Jimmie together we have no idea how much time has passed between the end of Act 1 Scene 1 and the beginning of Act 1 Scene 2, and Shelagh Delaney never tells us. Similarly, later in the same scene, we have no means of knowing how much time has elapsed between Christmas and Helen's marriage to Peter. When we next see Jo, it is summertime and she is with

Geof, but we have no idea how long she has known him. Then there is the curious time sequence you might have noted when Geof is cleaning the flat at the start of Act 2 Scene 2. It is obviously filthy and has not been properly cleaned since he moved in – he even finds Jo's bulbs under the sofa. Yet the stage direction tells us that several months have passed between this scene and the previous one in which Geof at one point told Jo he would clean the flat for her. We know that Geof is almost obsessively neat and tidy, and would hardly have been happy living in a dirty flat for several months. By such devices as these, Shelagh Delaney creates 'theatrical time' which produces a dreamlike effect and emphasizes that what we are seeing is drama, not life. It exists alongside a more normal time-scale which we can follow by observing the development of Jo's pregnancy.

The time at which *A Taste of Honey* was written was an important one for English drama, and for English novels too. After decades of dealing with the lives and manners of the English middle classes, plays and novels began to concentrate on working class characters. Playwrights like John Osborne and Arnold Wesker, and novelists like John Braine and Alan Sillitoe were in conscious rebellion against what they considered to be the smug, middle class values of earlier writing. It was their intention to shift the ground of literature and drama so that it exposed the class system in England, while at the same time showing that the lives of working class people were every bit as complex and interesting as those of their middle class counterparts. Some of these writers strove to be politically and socially provocative. In *Look Back In Anger* (1956), for example, John Osborne tried to show through his working class hero, Jimmy Porter, just how stifling middle class values were to those striving for change.

Shelagh Delaney did not write *A Taste of Honey* to protest about social conditions (although we can't help but notice the deprived area in which it is set). Even so, her assumption that the lives of working class people are a fit subject for a play shows her to be part of this broad 1950s movement. Born into a working class background herself, she wrote about what she knew, or could easily imagine from her knowledge of Salford. In his review of the play in July 1958, Lindsay Anderson wrote: 'Going north in Britain is always like a trip into another country, and *A Taste of Honey* is a real escape from the middlebrow, middle class vacuum of the West End.' Had the play been written twenty years earlier, it is doubtful that it would have been staged at all, let alone enjoyed great success, simply because characters like Jo and Helen were not considered worthy of serious dramatic presentation.

Question and assignment

Draw up a rough time chart for the play and fit an outline of the action to it. You can start in this way if you like.

Autumn/Early winter   – Jo and Helen move into flat.
pre-Christmas   – Jo and Jimmie engaged.

Assignment

Write a brief essay on time in *A Taste of Honey*.

Language

Shelagh Delaney catches very successfully the way people speak, and it is this authenticity which helps makes the play such a success. For example, we all sometimes change abruptly from one topic to another in mid-conversation, and this is something Helen does, especially in Act 1 Scene 1 when she is complaining about her cold and talking to Jo about the flat. Helen's language is also coloured with proverbs and slang, as much everyday speech is. Her third speech in the play has a proverbial ring about it, and her slang comment to Geof in Act 2 Scene 1 that he should sling his hook is much more realistic, and effective, than if she had simply asked him to leave.

As well as giving the play a sense of ordinary reality, the colloquialisms and slang expressions also reveal important details about the characters. For example, in Act 1 Scene 1, although Peter often uses slang, he frequently speaks in a rather sophisticated way – look for instance, at the speech in which he tells Helen that the world is littered with women he has rejected. Later, in Act 2 Scene 1, his deterioration is evident not only in his drunken behaviour, but in the coarse slang he speaks. The vulgarity of his language is one of the key ways of showing the unpleasantness of his character. In the same way, Jo's reliance on slang is a way of reflecting the influence of her mother. But like her mother, Jo does not rely entirely on slang; she shows a breadth of language usage which further demonstrates a similarity with Helen. They are both capable of scathing wit, for example. Jo's sardonic comment about the courtship of Peter and Helen is very reminiscent in its style and grasp of vocabulary of some of Helen's remarks. Wit is a weapon Jo has acquired from her mother and which she uses against her in their constant verbal battles.

Whereas slang and colloquialisms can quickly become stale and second-hand, wit requires an ability to express ideas briefly, humorously and with originality. It relies on a quick mind and a ready vocabulary. Neither Jo nor Helen is constantly witty – and this is again realistic – but their capacity to be so shows a mental agility which makes them more interesting and resourceful as characters.

Question and assignment

Make a list with these headings: Wit/Good Vocabulary, Slang/Colloquialism, Contemporary References. Then write down examples of each indicating who is speaking. This will give you a clear idea of the range of language in the play.

Assignment

Imagine that you are adapting *A Taste of Honey* as a novel. Produce your version of Act 1 Scene 1 down to where there is a loud bang. Remember that you must include description as well as dialogue and that you will not simply copy out exactly what Jo and Helen say to each other.

Humour and sadness

The play is a poignant blend of humour and sadness; not only do comic incidents alternate with more serious ones, but frequently incidents are both amusing and sombre at the same time. The early part of Act 2 Scene 2 provides us with a good example of the alternation of the comic and the serious; the scene begins lightheartedly enough, with Jo and Geof teasing each other, and with Geof pushing her playfully with the map. The accent here is upon the gentleness of the humour. Moments later, the discovery of the dead bulbs prompts Jo to reflect upon the haphazard nature of creation, that is, the casual, accidental way in which she, and her baby, have both come into being. The thought frightens her, and her sudden horror at such arbitrariness is all the more telling because of her happiness a little earlier. The pattern is immediately repeated. Geof reassures her with a mixture of jokes and assumed anger, but her recurring preoccupation with her father's sanity soon emerges once more and her good humour subsides.

On the majority of occasions, though, humour and sadness co-exist in the play. Let's look at some of the different types of humour before considering how they carry more sombre undertones. When we consider the humour more closely we see that it relies, to a great extent, on the techniques of variety shows, techniques which are often used in situation comedies on the television. Some examples will make this clear. You have probably seen situation comedies where the humour lies in the deflating of one of the characters. Characters make an exaggerated claim about themselves only to have another character puncture the boast and make them look silly. Think of the way, in Act 1 Scene 2, that Jo deflates Helen's boasting comments about her figure.

Another cherished device from variety shows is the quarrel between a threesome in which one of the participants suddenly and unexpectedly changes sides. This happens with bewildering speed in Act 2 Scene 1 when Helen visits, so that the effect is rather like slapstick comedy. At first it seems to be Helen and Geof versus Jo. Then they change as Helen and Jo seem to unite against Geof. Moments later, Helen sides with Geof once more, and so on. It is a humorous situation in which nobody seems quite clear as to who they should be arguing with, but at the same time it reveals the complexity of the characters and the contradictions in their feelings for one another.

Two other staple ingredients of comedy shows are the loud bang or crash off stage, and the comic drunk. Think of the occasions when you have seen a comedy programme on the television in which there has been the offscreen noise of an accident. Similarly, in *A Taste of Honey*, there is the loud bang when the gas stove explodes, followed by Jo's deadpan comment, and later Peter's drunken crashing in the kitchen. Peter himself is reminiscent of a stage drunk, singing, falling about, finding his own jokes vastly amusing, quite unaware of the effect he is having on others.

You can see, then, that much of the comedy of *A Taste of Honey* originates in the comedy of variety shows, which itself relies on certain stereotyped incidents, characters and comic deflations. What is interesting about Shelagh Delaney's play is that even though it is undeniably funny, the comic devices are used to illustrate its fundamental sadness. The witty interchanges between Helen and Jo, for instance, reveal their need to put each other down, to try to dominate or humiliate each other. And while the quarrel between Jo, Geof and Helen has many of the aspects of farce, we do not forget that it not only demonstrates the cruelty which Jo and Helen can show towards each other, it also warns us of the way in which Helen easily dominates Geof. As for the loud bangs, the first occurs because Helen is too negligent to help Jo light the stove and casually tells her to turn all the knobs on, and the second occurs because Peter can only cope with his inability to form relationships by getting drunk. Remember that when he emerges from the kitchen for the second time, he is even more unpleasant than he was previously.

Questions and assignments

1 Which scene do you find the saddest in the play?

2 Under the headings Actions and Speech make a list of some of the most comic incidents in the play so that you gain an idea of how much of the comedy is verbal and how much visual.

Relationships

The different kinds of relationship people have with each other as they seek for happiness – for a taste of honey – is one of the main concerns in the play. You might find it helpful to group these different kinds into categories because that will help you to compare and contrast them. One way of doing it is to divide them into three groups: couples, parent and child, and others.

Couples

This category deals with men and women who live together or have affairs with each other. You will see immediately that it comprises Jo and Jimmie, Jo and Geof, Helen and Peter. But it also includes Helen and her first husband, Helen and Jo's father, as well as Peter and the girl he has an affair with. Although we are not directly shown any of these relationships, we learn a great deal from the mention of them, especially about Peter and Helen. Such relationships help to define more sharply the focus of the play, so that we see how Helen demands sexual pleasure from any relationship with a man (contrast Jo), and how Peter soon tires of being married to an older woman and finds consolation in girls younger than himself.

All of these relationships, those we see and those we are told about, have one element in common: they do not last. They cover a time span from Helen's afternoon love affair with Jo's father through Peter's fortnight with a young girl to the longer, but finally broken, relationship Jo has with Geof. Obviously Shelagh Delaney attaches great importance to the fact that they all break down. As we read the play, we are confronted with characters seeking happiness, usually finding it for a while – but not always (think of Helen and her first husband) – and then having to pay a heavy price for it. Only Jimmie seems to escape without having to accept the consequences of what he does, and if we bear in mind that he will be the father of a child he will never know and never see, then perhaps he does not escape so lightly after all.

On the one occasion when a relationship (that of Jo and Geof) seems to have a chance of success it is spoiled by Helen's return. Looked at this way, the play is quite definitely pessimistic in its portrayal of human relationships. Shelagh Delaney seems to be suggesting that people are more likely to be disappointed than fulfilled in their relationships with each other. Often they seem to sense this and so desperately snatch at happiness without considering the consequences of what they are doing. Jo, Helen, and even Peter, offer ready examples of this.

There are, naturally, dissimilarities in the relationships outlined earlier. In this way the play avoids repetition. Jimmie and Peter, for example, are both sexually attracted to their partners, but Peter's open fondling of Helen, and his dirty jokes, show us how he sees Helen less as a woman than as an object of sexual satisfaction. Jimmie makes no secret of the fact that he desires Jo but he seems to care for her as well. The women, also, are attracted to different qualities in their men. Jo, at first anyway, romaticizes Jimmie, while Helen is attracted to Peter because he is young, rich and blatantly sexual.

The couple who have a relationship different from all the others is, of course, Jo and Geof. It is not only the most stable, although they often quarrel with each other, it is the one in which sex is almost entirely absent. We notice also that money, which plays a prominent role in Peter's relationship with Helen, also has no part in it. It functions as a satisfactory relationship because, as we saw when we studied their characters, Jo and Geof come to an understanding which answers the needs of both of them: he makes no demands on Jo, which pleases her because sex has lost its mystery and its attraction for her; she makes no demands on Geof and so eases his own sexual confusion.

Parent and Child

Because the relationship between Jo and Helen is the deepest and the most enduring in the play, the temptation is to think that this category is comprised solely of these two characters. In fact, it is the most all-embracing category in the play, for it overlaps the previous one as well. Think about this for a moment and you will realize that as well as Jo and Helen we have: Jo and her baby, Peter and Jo, Peter and Helen, Geof and Jo, Jimmie and Jo, Jo and her father, Helen and her mother. Once more you will see that several of these do not actually feature directly in the play – that is, we are not shown them – but as with the couples , these 'offstage' relationships serve to deepen the play's study of human nature. Let's look briefly at how Shelagh Delaney presents these variations upon the parent/child relationship in the play.

Helen freely admits that she is a failure as a mother. She further admits that Jo's conception and birth were a mistake. Jo is therefore very much an unwanted child and examples of Helen's resentment towards Jo are plentiful. However, Helen finds it difficult to cast Jo off entirely. When she learns of Jo's pregnancy, she visits her, brings her money and says she has been unable to sleep for worrying about her. Finally, when her marriage with Peter fails, it is to Jo that she returns. For her part, Jo also resents her mother and wishes to be independent of her. Yet she hates Peter because of the threat he represents to her, and in Act 2 Scene 2 she tells Geof that she wishes Helen were there. This bond between mother and daughter, unsatisfactory though it is, survives all manner of cruelty between them.

We see Jo not only as a daughter but also as a prospective mother. The similarity between her circumstances and Helen's is apparent to us straight away – and it is not accidental. It is an example of the way that Helen's negligence as a parent leads to a continuation of the cycle – unhappy home, brief affair, pregnancy. It is worth remembering that we are given a glimpse of Helen as a daughter, too, when she tells Jo in Act 1 Scene 1 that her mother would have beaten her for being rude to her. We sense from this that Helen's childhood was unhappy and made her take her pleasure wherever she could find it, just as Jo does with Jimmie. Both women enjoy their taste of honey; both are left pregnant.

Jo's attitude towards her baby swings violently from a sense of fulfilment to deep resentment. In Act 2 Scene 2, for example, we notice her pride in her comments to Geof. A little later she rages that she does not want a baby because it will propel her into womanhood before she is ready. Later still, though, she says that being pregnant has made her feel important for the first time in her life. By the end she seems to have accepted her role as mother, and so presents a contrast to Helen.

To include Geof and Jimmie in this category might seem odd at first, but we soon realize that there is a parental side to their relationships with Jo. When Jimmie comes to the flat in Act 1 Scene 2 we see him caring for Jo – rather as a loving parent might do for a sick child, but as Helen has never done. It is in Geof, however, that Jo finds someone who behaves most consistently like a mother to her. In cooking for her, cleaning the flat, and making baby clothes he takes on what should be Helen's role and provides Jo with the attention and security which Helen has never given her. But Geof has another role in this treatment of parent/child relationships. In a curious way, he is not only a kind of mother to Jo, but is an expectant father too. Although the baby is not his, he keenly awaits its birth and is quite willing to take responsibility for it.

This provides a clear contrast with Peter, who by marrying Helen becomes Jo's stepfather, but never shows the least concern for her. Just as he fails in his marriage to Helen, so he fails to establish a satisfactory relationship with Jo. In fact, rather than see himself as a father to Jo, he tends to see himself as Helen's son – in Act 1 Scene 1 he tells her that he likes their mother/son relationship, and in Act 1 Scene 2 tells Geof that he is like Oedipus, the Greek hero who unknowingly married his mother.

Although Jo never meets her father, Helen's story that he was retarded causes Jo great suffering as it makes her concerned for her own sanity as well as for her child's. It provides yet another example of the anxiety and bitterness which the majority of parent/child relationships in the play carry with them. Oddly enough, the most satisfactory of these relationships, excluding Jo's with her unborn child, is not a blood-tie (Helen/Jo, Helen/Helen's mother, Jo/Jo's father), or even a legal one (Peter/Jo). It is the emotional and temperamental bond between Jo and Geof.

Others

Two other relationships deserve a brief mention: Peter and Geof, and Helen and Geof. Peter's coarse manner to Geof confirms the difficulty he has in making satisfactory relationships except those of a crudely sexual kind. He makes no effort to understand how Geof has helped Jo, but merely resorts to drunken insults about Geof's homosexuality.

Helen, too, is convinced that Geof is a homosexual, and she finds him repulsive. However, she is not as obsessed by this as

Peter is. Like Peter, though, she shows no gratitude to Geof for caring for her daughter. Instead, determined to have her own way as always, she completely overwhelms him in a torrent of criticism of the way he looked after Jo.

Questions and assignments

1 How different is Jo's relationship with Jimmie from her relationship with Geof? Are there any similarities? Draw up a list under two headings: Geof and Jimmie.

2 Write down those relationships which we are told of but do not actually see. Then write two or three paragraphs explaining why they are important to the play.

Assignments

1 How convincing do you find the portrayal of Helen's relationship with Jo?

2 Imagine that you are Jimmie. What is your opinion of Jo?

General questions and coursework assignments

1 Write about how the title of the play applies to Jo and Helen.

Guideline answer

Important similarities in their reasons for wishing for a taste of honey, but some marked differences also which help distinguish them as characters.

Suggestion of Helen's unhappy childhood; certainty of her unhappy marriage. This leads her to seek happiness wherever she can find it. First of all with Jo's father. Brief, afternoon affair which gave her genuine, if momentary, fulfilment. Price she pays – conception of Jo – seems out of proportion to any sin committed. Thereafter seeks pleasure with men and drink. Marries Peter because rich and young. Gives little thought to his suitability. When marriage over seems to accept that any taste of honey is fleeting and followed by disappointment.

Like Helen, Jo seeks first taste of honey because of unhappiness. Like Helen pays the price of unwanted pregnancy. Unlike Helen, in that does not love her partner when sleeps with him. Unlike Helen also in that becomes uninterested in sex, finding deepest happiness in non-sexual relationship with Geof.

Whereas Helen's idea of taste of honey remains at the level of the physical and the material – drink, money, sex – Jo finds warmly satisfying period of fulfilment with Geof. It is based on mutual affection and understanding of each other's needs: Jo's for emotional support; Geof's for non-sexual relationship.

2 Compare Shelagh Delaney's use of setting in *A Taste of Honey* with the setting of any other play or book you have read. You might wish to choose one with a similar background such as *Kes* or *Love on the Dole* or you can if you like select something entirely different, such as Corfu in *My Family and Other Animals*.

3 The local newspaper is running a series of profiles on housing and the environment. Write the article dealing with Jo's flat and the area in which it is situated.

4 In an earlier form of the play, the marriage of Peter and Helen seems to work out quite well. In fact, Peter confesses to

Helen that he really likes children, and suggests, just before they visit Jo, that they should take care of Jo's baby, and Jo herself. Write, in play form, either the scene in which he talks to Helen or the scene in which Helen and he try to persuade Jo to live with them.

5 In the original version, Jo is taken to hospital, while Geof is out, to have her baby. When he returns, he and Helen have a long discussion in which he comes to accept that Jo will live with her mother when the baby is born. The play ends with Geof left alone in the flat holding the doll. Write this version as a play.

6 Imagine that you are Geof. Write a letter to Jo three months after you left explaining how you feel about her, and why you decided to leave.

7 Compare the argument Helen and Jo have in Act 2 Scene 1 with any other argument between a parent and a child in a book you have read. Be sure to bring out any similarities or differences.

8 Write an account of what happens to Peter after Helen leaves.

9 Imagine that you are one of Jo's neighbours. Give your account of what happens in the play based upon what you are likely to see and hear.

10 Which relationship do you find the most interesting in the play?

11 Imagine that you are Jo. What will you tell your baby about Jimmie?

12 Write a piece which either compares or contrasts Jo with any other fictional heroine. (You can choose someone very different, like Ann in *Z for Zachariah* or Scout in *To Kill a Mockingbird*, or someone who is more similar, like Holden Caulfield in *Catcher in the Rye*).

13 Compare or contrast Helen's attitude to marriage with that of any other character in a book you have read.

14 The play was written in the 1950s. Do you think it is still relevent today?

15 Do you like or dislike Helen? Give reasons for your view of her.

Pan study aids Titles published in the Brodie's Notes series

Edward Albee Who's Afraid of Virginia Woolf?

W. H. Auden Selected Poetry

Jane Austen Emma Mansfield Park Northanger Abbey Persuasion
Pride and Prejudice

Anthologies of Poetry Ten Twentieth Century Poets The Poet's Tale
The Metaphysical Poets

Samuel Beckett Waiting for Godot

Arnold Bennett The Old Wives' Tale

William Blake Songs of Innocence and Experience

Robert Bolt A Man for All Seasons

Harold Brighouse Hobson's Choice

Charlotte Brontë Jane Eyre Villette

Emily Brontë Wuthering Heights

Bruce Chatwin On the Black Hill

Geoffrey Chaucer (parallel texts editions) The Franklin's Tale
The Knight's Tale The Miller's Tale The Nun's Priest's Tale
The Pardoner's Tale Prologue to the Canterbury Tales
The Wife of Bath's Tale

John Clare Selected Poetry and Prose

Gerald Cole Gregory's Girl

Wilkie Collins The Woman in White

Joseph Conrad Heart of Darkness The Nigger of the Narcissus
Youth

Daniel Defoe Journal of a Plague Year

Shelagh Delaney A Taste of Honey

Charles Dickens David Copperfield Dombey and Son
Great Expectations Hard Times Little Dorrit Oliver Twist
Our Mutual Friend

Gerald Durrell My Family and Other Animals

George Eliot Middlemarch The Mill on the Floss Silas Marner

T. S. Eliot Murder in the Cathedral Selected Poems

J. G. Farrell The Siege of Krishnapur

W. Faulkner As I lay Dying

Henry Fielding Joseph Andrews Tom Jones

F. Scott Fitzgerald The Great Gatsby

E. M. Forster Howards End A Passage to India

E. Gaskell North and South

William Golding Lord of the Flies Rites of Passage The Spire

Oliver Goldsmith Two Plays of Goldsmith: She Stoops to Conquer;
The Good Natured Man

Graham Greene Brighton Rock The Human Factor
The Power and the Glory The Quiet American

Willis Hall The Long and the Short and the Tall

Thomas Hardy Chosen Poems of Thomas Hardy
Far from the Madding Crowd The Mayor of Casterbridge
Return of the Native Tess of the d'Urbervilles The Trumpet-Major
The Woodlanders

L. P. Hartley The Go-Between The Shrimp and the Anemone

Joseph Heller Catch-22

Ernest Hemingway A Farewell to Arms

Susan Hill I'm the King of the Castle

Barry Hines Kes

Aldous Huxley Brave New World

Henry James Washington Square

Ben Jonson Volpone

James Joyce A Portrait of the Artist as a Young Man Dubliners

John Keats Selected Poems and Letters of John Keats

D. H. Lawrence The Rainbow Sons and Lovers

Harper Lee To Kill a Mockingbird

Laurie Lee Cider with Rosie

Thomas Mann Death in Venice & Tonio Kröger

Christopher Marlowe Doctor Faustus Edward the Second

W. Somerset Maugham Of Human Bondage

Gavin Maxwell Ring of Bright Water

Thomas Middleton The Changeling

Arthur Miller The Crucible Death of a Salesman

John Milton A Choice of Milton's Verse Comus and Samson Agonistes Paradise Lost I, II

Bill Naughton Spring and Port Wine

R. O'Brien Z for Zachariah

Sean O'Casey Juno and the Paycock
The Shadow of a Gunman and the Plough and the Stars

George Orwell Animal Farm 1984

John Osborne Luther

Alexander Pope Selected Poetry

J. B. Priestley An Inspector Calls

J. D. Salinger The Catcher in the Rye

Siegfried Sassoon Memoirs of a Fox-Hunting Man

Peter Shaffer The Royal Hunt of the Sun

William Shakespeare Antony and Cleopatra As You Like It
Coriolanus Hamlet Henry IV (Part I) Henry IV (Part II) Henry V
Julius Caesar King Lear Love's Labour's Lost Macbeth Measure for
Measure The Merchant of Venice A Midsummer Night's Dream
Much Ado about Nothing Othello Richard II Richard III Romeo and
Juliet The Sonnets The Taming of the Shrew The Tempest Twelfth
Night The Winter's Tale

G. B. Shaw Pygmalion Saint Joan

Richard Sheridan Plays of Sheridan: The Rivals; The Critic;
The School for Scandal

John Steinbeck The Grapes of Wrath Of Mice and Men The Pearl

Tom Stoppard Rosencrantz and Guildenstern are Dead

Jonathan Swift Gulliver's Travels

J. M. Synge The Playboy of the Western World

Dylan Thomas Under Milk Wood

Flora Thompson Lark Rise to Candleford

Anthony Trollope Barchester Towers

Mark Twain Huckleberry Finn

Keith Waterhouse Billy Liar

John Webster The Duchess of Malfi The White Devil

H. G. Wells The History of Mr Polly The War of the Worlds

Oscar Wilde The Importance of Being Earnest

William Wordsworth The Prelude (Books 1, 2)

William Wycherley The Country Wife

W. B. Yeats Selected Poetry

GCSE English coursework: Prose G. Handley and P. Wilkins

GCSE English coursework: Drama and Poetry: K. Dowling

PAN STUDY AIDS – GCSE

▶ The complete guide to GCSE exam success

▶ Authors, highly experienced teachers, examiners and writers in every case, have taken account of ALL syllabuses in their subjects

▶ GCSE Study Aids cover all the essentials, focusing on the areas which carry the most marks and paying particular attention to common points of difficulty

▶ GCSE Study Aids supply expert guidance on how to revise and prepare for the exams

▶ GCSE Study Aids illustrate the varied types of exam questions, explaining exactly what examiners look for

▶ GCSE Study Aids give students the chance to practise their answers using sample questions supplied by the examination boards.

Books in the series: